OWN
MASTER YOUR CHARACTER
YOUR
RISE TO ANY CHALLENGE
SELF
FIND TRUE INNER PEACE

CARY HOKAMA

Copyright © 2018 by Cary Hokama

Own Your Self: Master Your Character, Rise to Any Challenge, and Find True Inner Peace

All rights reserved. No part of this publication may be reproduced, distributed, or transmitted in any form or by any means, including photocopying, recording, or other electronic or mechanical methods, without the prior written permission of the publisher, except in the case of brief quotations embodied in critical reviews and certain other noncommercial uses permitted by copyright law. For permission requests, write to the publisher, addressed "Attention: Permissions Coordinator," at info@beyondpublishing.net

Quantity sales special discounts are available on quantity purchases by corporations, associations, and others. For details, contact the publisher at the address above.

Orders by U.S. trade bookstores and wholesalers. Email info@BeyondPublishing.net

The Beyond Publishing Speakers Bureau can bring authors to your live event. For more information or to book an event contact the Beyond Publishing Speakers Bureau speak@BeyondPublishing.net

The Author can be reached directly
BeyondPublishing.net/AuthorCaryHokama

Manufactured and printed in the United States of America distributed globally by BeyondPublishing.net

New York | Los Angeles | London | Sydney

10 9 8 7 6 5 4 3 2 1 978-1-947256-47-7

Acknowledgments

Aileen, you are perfect now and you were perfect when I met you. You are my heartbeat and I love you to bits and pieces. The best is yet to come :) Mom and Dad, thank you for your never ending love and sacrifice. My life is fulfilled because of your support. I love you guys with every inch of my heart. Marcy, you are the toughest girl I know. Though you're the younger sibling, you are my teacher and mentor. I look forward to our many trips to NY and hanging with Matt and Niko! I love you.

I have to say, I have the best in-laws! Thank you papa Moon, mama Moon, Sandy, and Philip. Your constant love and support is so greatly appreciated.

A huge thank you to the guys responsible for shaping my purpose: Yoshi Abe, Hendre Coetzee, Adam James, Mike DeMora, Mike "Mano" Wrice, Tory Woodward, Brian Jones, and Abe "The Babe" Lim. Thank you for investing in me when you didn't have to. I am eternally grateful to all of you!

The book squad: To my coaches Emily Rose and Chandler Bolt, you guys (and the rest of SPS) have no idea what we've started. This is only the beginning! Thank you and cheers! To my editor, Ari Fard, it was love at first "write" baby! Let's go back to back! Heidi Sutherlin and Christian Fuenfhausen, you guys are extremely gifted. Thank you for your immense talent!

24LG: We had a historic run, didn't we? I will never forget our 3 years of breaking bread and doing life together.

Modus Dei Fans: It's been 8 crazy years since we played our last show, but I will never forget the most amazing 7 years of my life. Thank you for supporting us and letting us rock our socks off in front of you! We obviously never "made it" but you guys made us feel like bona fide rock stars. More importantly, my experience as the front man has led me to do what I am doing today. So thank you from the bottom of my heart.

My Gracie Academy family: You are my second home. The journey is real and amazing. I learn from each and every one of you every time I step foot on the green mat. Muito obrigado!

Finally, to my past and present clients at NLF: You know who you are…your daily, weekly, and yearly commitment and participation is my greatest fuel and inspiration. Let's keep doing what we do…as long as y'all grind, I'll keep dancing!

A Message from the Author

I got sick and tired of losing. Disappointment after disappointment, I would find myself grappling with pity—asking myself, "When's it going to be my turn?" Vulnerable yet hopeful, in 2005, I decided to prevail over my downheartedness by using self-help books. My buddy, Yoshi, suggested that I read *How to Win Friends and Influence People* by Dale Carnegie—and the rest is history. Reading became a regal experience. I felt as if someone whiffed my brain with smelling salts—awakening my resting consciousness. When I read, I began to use my mind. When I started using my mind, I became primed to learn and to prepare. Once learning and preparation implanted themselves into my life, I began to win. I grew to understand and to appreciate more with each bit of information I absorbed. Suddenly books began enveloping my world. My cranial space became a forum for insatiable learning, interactive teaching, and personal growth. Books became my best friends and taught me more than the best teachers.

While self-help books kindled my desire in reading, its influence did not stop there. Currently, I obsess over personal development and self-improvement. Human behavior and potential continue to arouse my curiosities. I find myself navigating a maze, realizing that the more I know, the more I realize how much I don't know. This perpetual, mental treadmill drives my actions and keeps me yearning for knowledge every day.

I want you to know that this isn't just a book; every shared principle reflects how I live and how I prepare. The information I provide does not present an earth-shattering message, but rather a collage of information. A collection of knowledge I amassed by learning from global leaders and those dedicated to teaching and inspiring others.

Within this text, I share my most personal stories and unique experiences. To effectively utilize the tools I share in this book, I implore you to open your mind and to awaken your desire to learn and participate. I am indebted to those of you who picked up this book, but I am filled with gratitude to those who apply the principles taught hereafter. We do not experience life solitarily, we embark on the journey together.

Contents

Acknowledgments i
A Message from the Author iv
Introduction 1

Chapter 1 9
Step 1: Mastering the Mind 9

Chapter 2 48
Step 2: Nutrition - Master your food 48

Chapter 3 76
Step 3: Master Your Fitness & Body 76

Chapter 4 92
Step 4: Master Your Wealth & Success 92

Chapter 5 107
Step 5: Master of Giving 107

Chapter 6 118
Final Words 118

Introduction

"Everyone dies, but how many of us truly live?"
—Unknown

If you died today, what would your gravestone say? How would you be remembered by those closest to you? Would your eulogy sound something like: "Here lies Cary—an ambitious husband filled with endless opportunities. Cary's life comprised of many talents and skills; however, his fears disabled him from taking the risks and sacrifices necessary for actualizing his potential. Everyone liked his personality so many people wished to work and partner alongside him. Unfortunately, the repeated wounds from being hurt caused him to live the rest of his life in isolation. May he rest in peace."

Nobody wants to be remembered as an unfulfilled potential—festering in the sun like an abandoned dream. Hopefully, your eulogy sounds a bit more like this: "Here lies Cary—an ambitious husband, loyal brother, and amazing son. Filled with endless potential, Cary's gravestone cannot encompass the magnitude of his life story or his accomplishments. His passion fueled the lives of those around him— igniting enthusiasm in any room he entered. The harmony between his playful nature and astounding work bedazzled everyone. He loved, lived, and gave with all of his heart. He accomplished his mission and his family misses him dearly."

The greatest gift that you can give to this world is yourself. By achieving your full potential, you create an inspiring life worth sharing. Nobody on Earth can mirror the qualities that make you, you, thus life's ultimate achievement occurs when you act like yourself.

Sadly, many times the complexity of life undermines your potential and dilutes the person you transpire to be. You desperately try to adapt but find that your struggle creates a bigger disconnect. A previous client of mine used to sign off—ending all of his emails with the quote, "Pain is mandatory, misery is optional." He got the point. Life births pain, however, the toughest struggles yield the greatest triumphs. Taking responsibility for your endeavors and overcoming adversity rewards your resolve with a unique sense of joy and fulfillment.

Responding to your abilities and interacting with your choices characterizes your identity. People think they're too fat, too old, not beautiful enough or consistently short on time: evidence exists for all of these beliefs. Giving into these *voices* manifests a reality that chisels away at your identity. Remember that your parents really never cared for you? Remember that person who cheated on you?

Remember your boss who doesn't like you? All of these beliefs act in parallel to your life. It's written on your face and evident in your personality. Giving in to these thoughts creates a recurring problem of repeated behaviors that entangles your life. You end up making the same bad business decisions, making the same mistakes in relationships, and having the same fights with your spouse, children, or loved ones. Fortunately, if channeled correctly, this conflict can encourage change: by creating tension, people begin to feel a stimulus—generating an opportunity for transformation.

As a Transformation Specialist and Fitness Professional, people ask me, "What do I do Cary? How do I get the energy you have and what do I need to do to get awesome results fast?" If I could encode their question into how I hear it, their plea sounds like, "Here you go Cary. Here is my money. Now fix me quickly." When clients approach me with this mentality, it clearly signals a disconnect within their beliefs.

People don't want to transform; instead, they yearn for affirmation. They want someone to listen to their grievances and say, "Yes, you are right." People pacify their shortcomings by seeking reassurance from others. Parents reaffirm their five-year-old by telling them that they have potential. Even telling a twenty-five-year-old that they have potential can also pass as an affirmation. However, once you pass the age of twenty-five, assertions become accusations. If someone tells you that you have potential, it becomes your responsibility to fulfill that accusation.

We love the idea of potential because of the possibilities. People hope that one day their ideal self will bloom into fruition and become just as tangible as an orange on a tree. However, any undesirable aspect of your life exists due to your lack of participation. Facilitating change and transformation requires active participation. You need to change you! Transformation occurs when you engage your life on different terms. We all see our potential yet somehow resist fulfilling it. Comfort zones lock us into regular routines that disengage us from life's obstacles and challenges.

Your journey forward does not focus on the past. This battle does not involve your significant other, parents, or friends. Your battle should address the effort needed in making breakthrough achievements. We live within a culture that worships understanding; however, understanding is just an illusion of transformation. Commitment and hard work drive people toward success. People's fears often emerge during the process; however, I do not intend to eliminate a client's fears. *Fearless* does not mean the absence of fear; fearless means that you do not allow fear to govern your life. Act courageously and progress through life in spite of fear.

I created a 5-in-1-step developmental process to facilitate holistic personal transformations. Your *craft* is your character and the *challenge* is your life's obstacles. I included the word "holistic" because of the homogeneity of human nature. The physical universe does not lie, and you will achieve tasks proportionate to the effort that you put in. You are a human being and your *being* is the union of your beliefs.

Learning to develop into the best versions of ourselves constitutes my standard of success. My process encourages readers to actively pursue their highest level of human potential. This level of self-mastery allows you to live an extraordinary life filled with fulfillment and inspired action. I'm not here to change your future; instead, I hope to change the current so that you can dynamically engage with the future.

The 5-in-1 steps provide an in-depth process, which includes 5 sub-components in each of the steps. I've broken the system down into practical methods so that by the end of this book, you will learn how to master the following areas:

Mastering Your Mind

- Reality Check
- Vision and Purpose
- Mastering Your Inner-Conversation
- Participation and Commitment
- Law of Attraction

Mastering Your Nutrition

- Lifestyle vs Diet

- Proper supplementation
- Proper water and fat intake
- My personal secret of always staying fit and lean

Mastering Your Body

- Mind connection & control
- 5 Components of Fitness
- Integrating Jiu-Jitsu / Martial Arts / Yoga into your life

Mastering Your Wealth & Success

- Your personal belief about money
- Know your passion
- Networking with great mentors
- Minimize Risk, Maximize Opportunity
- Integrity and gratitude.

Mastery of Giving

- Forgiving
- Improving Relationships
- Give your time
- Give your money
- Serve unconditionally

To liberate yourself, you need to face your fears and actively participate. My dear friend and mentor, Hendre Coetzee, always said that we have the tendency to find a comfortable level of despair and call it happiness. When will the despair finally become unbearable? Tony Robbins said, "When will now be a good time? When will you say, now?" Don't tell me that you're busy. We're all busy. Do not find a way to justify your fears. Jim Rohn always preached that a life of progress equals happiness, so take these skills I lay out and progress towards happiness. You deserve it and people deserve you. Your greatness lies ahead. Let's jump on in.

Chapter 1
Step 1: Mastering the Mind

1st Component: Reality Check

*"Always remember to fall asleep
with a dream and wake up with a purpose"*
— **Unknown**

Life's a bitch. It can be harsh and extremely unfair. I know hearing this won't help, but it's the life you settled for. It's all on you and nobody else. Your actions dictate where you are in life. That's reality.

Every day I wake up at 4 A.M. I sit up on my bed, and say to myself, "I'm up, I'm thankful to be alive. Thank you, God, that I'm alive and that I have a purpose today. Let's make today count." I start each morning with sincere gratitude and reflection; however, I also remind myself to be acutely aware that I am one day closer to my death.

I know it sounds quite strange, but mortality motivates my daily actions: it gets me to do things and drives me to get stuff done. I realize that my clock consistently ticks forward and that I can literally die at any time. For that reason, I live life to its fullest and acknowledge that now is the time to be great. I know it may sound a bit dramatic, but I really do leverage death so that I can live the best life possible. Every morning before I leave the house, I kiss my wife, Aileen, goodbye. As I leave, I comprehend that this could be the last time I ever kiss or see her again. I don't want to sound like a downer, but this concept of death and mortality seriously drives me to be the greatest husband I can be. If I get to see another day, I will treat it just the same.

The same goes when I think about my loved ones, my friends, and my coworkers. I'm dead serious. Life is precious and so unpredictable. A few weeks ago, the police found my friend Chuck strangled to death in his own car. Chuck sold rare tennis shoes, so people suspected that his death resulted from a regrettable transaction. Maybe it was a drug deal, who knows? Do you think Chuck knew of his impending departure? No way, right? He drove to the hotel hoping to profit off of some shoes! How we utilize our time defines everything. I am humbled by time and death every day.

A few years ago, I attended a private gathering of the most influential business and non-profit leaders in New York City. There, I had the opportunity to sit ten feet away from iconic thought leader and author, Erwin McManus. At some point, Mr. McManus stood up and shared, "Your life is like a bottle of wine. It can never be perfect, and it will never be perfect because it can only be beautiful. The only way to die a good death is to live a good life." I know it sounds like a cheesy line from Forrest Gump, but these words blasted my thoughts with profound ideas.

Let me ask you this: does your own story keep you from progressing? Does this narrative hold you back from breakthrough? How can you overcome these deeply rooted mental barriers so that you can transform? The reality is, people like to learn, but they don't like to practically apply the things they learn. Everyone knows the saying *knowledge is power*, but everyone does not know that knowledge creates guilt. Unused knowledge means nothing; it means nothing because when knowledge becomes crippled by inaction, what function does it serve?

I want you to repeat this to yourself right now: "Where I am, is exactly where I want to be." Did you say it? Now, I want you to believe it in your heart. Please repeat it again. "Where I am, is exactly where I want to be." Now, repeat this to yourself with absolute conviction, "I am okay with where I am. I'm just too damn good to stay here."

Earlier I mentioned that your life reflects the life you settled for. Point A represents your current life and Point B indicates your breakthrough into a personal transformation. For simplicity, hereafter both conditions will be referred to as Point A or Point B. If you desire a different life, you will need to participate differently. My goal is to get you to point B so that you can live an extraordinary life full of inspired action.

Accept full responsibility for everything. The decisions you make represent the life you live and accountability acts as a reality check. It's time for self-ownership. Not only will I make you take complete ownership of yourself, but I will hold you responsible for where you're going as well. Transformation is a process of owning responsibility. I cannot manipulate it, but you can.

What does responsibility mean to you? What comes to mind when you hear responsibility? You may think, "I'm responsible for making money and paying the bills." Or, "I'm responsible for raising my children and giving them the best life possible." Whatever it may be, the point is that many things come to mind. My responsibilities include managing my business and ensuring customer satisfaction. The issue of responsibility is that people view it as a burden and duty rather than a vehicle towards empowerment.

Hendre taught me an invaluable application for responsibility. He instructed me to look at responsibility as two words: response and ability. You can think of it as responding to your abilities, or engaging in your abilities. You might react and say, "But Cary, I get this and I know what you're saying, but you just don't understand where I've been and what I've been through in my life. There is too much pain and just too many things that need to be fixed." Yes, you're right and I'm sorry. Your journey paints a sacred and personal portrait that I may not understand. Nevertheless, I ask you to look into whatever you believe and explore the effects of those beliefs. I certainly understand pain and emotional hurt. I also realize the difficulty of healing your past while concurrently coping with current issues. People try to reconcile their past by completely forgetting about it. I think the best way to deal with your past is by forming a dynamic relationship with your future (Point B).

When you drive, why do you use the rear-view mirror? For safety? I would say that you use the rear-view mirror to gain a different perspective while driving. What would happen if you drove from Los Angeles to San Francisco only using the rear-view mirror? You would crash and get into an accident—right? The same idea applies to your life. When getting to Point B, it's crucial to check your rear-view mirror here and there; however, to reach your destination, you must look ahead and focus on your path forward. So let's go.

2ND COMPONENT: VISION & PURPOSE

"The two most important days in your life are the day you are born, and the day you found out why."
— Mark Twain

The Good Book says that where there is no vision, people perish. Jim Rohn said, "Life is not about how long you live but how you live." So, what is your life's work? What are your values? What are your God-given talents and skills? What do you stand for? What is your vision and ultimate purpose in life?

Everyone has the potential to create unprecedented possibilities, but it requires innovation, creativity, and designing new realities. You create new realities with your vision. It's your responsibility to breathe life into your soul and act upon it.

I believe in faith, I believe in love, and I believe in hard work. I believe in goodness and I believe in you. I can speak into your heart and bolster your spirit, but your own words hold the most influential power. How you envision your future determines how you participate in the present. Declare your possibilities and do whatever it takes to live up to that.

In the early 1960's, John F. Kennedy promised to put a man on the moon by decade's end. Think of how contextually asinine that sounded. Even NASA thought that the President had lost his mind. Whatever the case, JFK told NASA to figure it out, and they freaking figured it out! In fact, by the time Neil Armstrong landed on the moon, JFK had already passed away. The relevance of this story is that JFK depicted a vision that invoked national support and participation. His vision gave birth to an unprecedented possibility and it became a reality. Make your vision clear, dictate your future, and do the work required to get you there. A clear vision eliminates improbabilities and acts within the frame it requires.

Vision and purpose go hand in hand; they support one another like uncompromising allies. In the last several years, businesses and leadership groups popularized the role of a *visionary*. Now many companies hire a C.V.O., or Chief Visionary Officer, to help steer the company into a promising future. Visionaries can be defined as possibility thinkers. For many years, I considered myself a visionary. The problem with visionaries is that many of them don't have a vision. You can no longer just be a visionary—it's not enough.

A person with vision and purpose chooses one, and declares, "I'm going to go with this one." While he or she might not have many ways to get there, the vision itself does not change. Transformation and change frequently occur throughout this process; however, the closer you get to point B the clearer your vision becomes. You change, but the vision does not. JFK died in the process of actualizing his vision; what are you willing to do for your vision?

I would describe my life's journey as unique, event-filled, and entirely purposeful. My resume includes working as a waiter, sports TV producer, semi-rock star, eBay power-seller, recording studio owner, discount store owner, door-to-door salesman, telemarketer, sunglass brand manager, real estate agent, personal trainer, and missionary. On top of that, I have many memorable and random life experiences. In fact, Aileen and I filmed our wedding and had it televised on a reality show via the Oprah Winfrey Network. To go even further, my band and I headlined our last show in front of a sold-out crowd at the Roxy Theater in Hollywood.

Throughout my life, I knew that I was destined for something extraordinary, something great. My fire ignited from an early age. Not to sound cocky or arrogant, but since the age of seven, I could tangibly feel my feverous passion and mental drive. I wanted to make a significant impact in the world. Often, I would tell my parents that I was destined to become a famous actor, world-class musician, or pro athlete. The grandeur lives associated with those professions awed me. I considered Michael Jackson and Michael Jordan as my number one heroes. I studied both Michaels; mimicking their swagger, drive, and attitude. I immersed myself in their every move and watched them perform at the highest levels of professionalism. I made a commitment to myself that no matter what I did, I would be the absolute best at it. I had to showcase my skills and talents for a sea of people.

I got my first "real" job as an upperclassman in college. Fox Sports hired me as a production assistant, and I thought I was big time. Immediately after getting hired, I remember driving to Banana Republic and buying as many threads as my budget would allow. At the time, working for Fox Sports sounded like a dream job: I got to watch professional sports games all while getting paid. I wanted to become the hottest sports anchor in Southern California—making the Asian-American Community proud. I envisioned all of Los Angeles anxiously tuning into my network, as I entertained them with daily sports highlights. Unfortunately, after a year and a half of stagnant and repetitive work, I found myself depressed, unhappy, and forty pounds heavier. I remember driving home at night thinking, "Is this really it?" Is this how I'm going to spend the next forty to fifty years of my life?

Feeling empty and unfulfilled, I came home and restlessly laid on my bed. I began to think about my childhood while an epiphanic moment of clarity defibrillated my mind. My dreams of performing on the world stage reawakened and my bedroom ceiling became a cinema reel of endless possibilities. This time, I knew that I would move thousands of people.

A week passed since I had that vision. Everything went back to normal until I suddenly received an unexpected call from a childhood friend. We caught up for a few minutes until he asked, "Dude, Cary, I know this is super random, but we just lost our lead singer. Would you like to audition for our band to replace him?" The question triggered a cascade of adrenaline that flooded through my body. The following week I quit my job at Fox Sports and decided to dedicate the next seven years of my life as Modus Dei's lead singer and front man.

I took a path toward my dream life by manifesting a childhood vision. I assumed that this random sequence of events was God's plan: I would become a rock-star and impact people's lives through my music. Modus Dei performed at L.A's best nightclubs. We made three albums over seven years, opened for many major touring acts, and sold out a Saturday night show at The Roxy Theatre in Hollywood. Unfortunately, music executives disregarded our many successes and overlooked our talent. They called us unmarketable and suggested that our music didn't have enough depth to make it in the industry. The record label ripped open my chest and extracted my heart with their criticism.

In early 2008, our band decided to break up and call it quits. It was heartbreaking because I thought I had finally found my passion. I thought, "why would my vision and passion be cut so abruptly and end with such ambivalence." Angry and miserable, I blamed everyone for everything that occurred. I was a confused thirty-year-old with no career. Desperately looking for work, I sank to a new low by taking a job as a door-to-door salesman. My 9 to 5 shift consisted of homeowners repeatedly slamming doors in my face. A few months before people swarmed me for autographs and pictures, but now people escaped me like the clap. I quit that job after 2 weeks.

In early 2012, I attended a workshop organized by Hendre Coetzee. Hendre is a world-class transformation specialist and a former South African hostage negotiator. I attended his coaching program as his sole "scholarship" student and never thought that he would impact my life the way he has. As the program came to an end, Hendre shared a story with us about the biblical figure, Samuel. Samuel was a kingmaker, and his work focused on finding and empowering kings for the following generations. Upon hearing this story, my life's purpose became apparent: I am a kingmaker. I spent my first thirty-three years trying to be a king, and now I will spend the next half of my life grooming the next kings and queens of our generation. I am Samuel.

As I write this book, I look back and think of all the obstacles I had to overcome in getting here. All of the pain, betrayal, and hardships prepared me as a mentor for others. Paving people's path toward an extraordinary life became my purpose. I want to elicit people's potentials and lead them towards a life of inspired action regardless of their circumstances. The process changed, I changed, but my vision and purpose never did. I believed in myself, I knew my goal, and I followed my path. I obsessed to become the best version of myself so that I could help others do the same.

Why do people buy lottery tickets? They buy it so that they can spend the next ten minutes fantasizing about a life of luxury. Haven't you done that before? I certainly have. A lottery ticket embodies a vision without responsibility—a fantasy. We fantasize in order to cope with difficult circumstances. It's an escape from reality. Ditch the lottery ticket mentality.

Recently, the country witnessed three winners from California, Florida, and Tennessee, claim a record Powerball jackpot of $1.6 Billion. It was mind blowing. Considering all of the pressure and nuisances involved in winning, I think the winners would be better off not winning at all. Their success symbolizes a miracle. Miracles do occur; however, they occur within a blip of your timeline. Don't get me wrong; miracles are beautiful, they're fantastic, but the ultimate goal rests upon how you commit to your future. The day your vision and purpose collide will become the 2nd most important day of your life. On that day, you find out *why* you were born.

Take it a step further. Most, if not all companies, have a mission statement. Their mission statement is equivalent to your "vision statement." Create one for yourself and write it down. After, dictate your purpose and write it down. It takes some time to nail, but as you continue working, your vision and purpose will come to you. I suggest pinning these statements on your wall so that you can see them daily. Great companies display their mission statement so that employees and customers can see their intent.

Here's mine:

My Vision Statement: To relentlessly pursue self-mastery and virtue. Love Aileen faithfully and serve my family unconditionally; do my work passionately and fulfill my

God-given purpose with humility; I want to be present & grateful for every moment. I live life purposefully and consciously by using inspired action. I appreciate my life regardless of my circumstances.

My Purpose: I am a Kingmaker. My life's purpose is to ADD VALUE to the lives of others. I achieve everything I desire and I never undermine myself by settling. I wish to propagate these skills to others so that I can help them accomplish anything they want. I will uphold the duty of building the next generation of kings and queens. Aileen and I will visit a new country or city every year, and we will develop communities that unify people.

Prioritize writing your vision and purpose down on paper. It doesn't have to be perfect but it's important that you see it and read it physically. It will quickly and drastically change your life!

3RD COMPONENT: MASTER YOUR INTERNAL-CONVERSATION

"Whatever you say you can, or whatever you say you can't, you're right."
— Confucius

You are not listening to me. You are listening to what you are telling yourself. People do not do what I say; they do what they say to themselves. You are a product of your internal dialogue because these conversations govern your actions. My job requires that you vocalize this internal dialogue. No matter what you reveal, everyone is capable of transformation. Your subconscious converses all the time. Research indicates that the average person thinks 50,000 to 60,000 thoughts a day! Can you imagine your cranial atmosphere? Considering that 70-80% of those thoughts are negative, it's a miracle that we can even function.

People consistently paralyze themselves with fear and a lack of confidence. Social media, pop culture, and television promote a culture that drowns our self-worth and authenticity. It's all trash; however the world does a spectacular job of making us buy into these lies. Tune all of that out. I want you to focus on the internal conversations you are having with yourself because these thoughts influence the way you behave. Your internal conversations whisper lies that create doubt. This leads to self-limiting beliefs.

A limiting belief empowers itself through secrecy. Don't be impaired by your limiting beliefs. The moment you uncover this hindering thought, it loses a significant amount of its power. Now that you identified your limiting belief, it can no longer govern you. What just happened when you revealed your limiting belief? You created a distance between yourself and that belief. You separated yourself from the lie. If you master your internal self, you will master your mind. If you master your internal dialogue, you will master your life. This is all part of the holistic transformation. New conversations do not always guarantee new actions, but new measures require new communication.

Everything you listen to or hear will be nothing but chatter. You must control the dialogue within your head. When a voice invades your thoughts, I want you to tune in carefully, "Who or what is in control?" "Who or what is governing my actions?" Is it truth? Or is it a lie? Vocalize your thought process. Recalibrate your language and thinking so that you can filter the truth from the lies. Act upon the truth and boldly step into action.

Despite his recent struggles, many still consider Tiger Woods as one of golf's all-time greats. According to Forbes, Woods became the first athlete to reach $1 Billion in career earnings! My knowledge of golf is mediocre at best; however, I always enjoyed watching Woods perform during championship tours. In my opinion, the greatest athletes have a particular trademark. Michael Jordan stuck out his tongue, Muhammad Ali confidently taunted his opponents, and David Beckham curved a soccer ball like a baseball pitcher.

Watching Woods throughout the years, I grew to admire his practical use of self-talk. Sometimes sports networks would connect him to a microphone—capturing all of his conversations for the day. Even on those days, Tiger would maintain his focus by utilizing positive self-talk. Tiger completely controlled his dialogue and dominated his way into becoming a winner and golf legend.

For many years, I battled and brawled against my inner-voices. It was a constant tug of war: sometimes I would gain ground, but on most days I took a beating. These voices carpet bombed my confidence with negativity, always reminding me of my inabilities and shortcomings. My insecurities got the best of me. My mom's voice would add to the polyphony, telling me to trade my dream for a safe and stable 9-to-5. To this day, I still laugh at the advice my mother gave me after my band broke up. She told me that I needed to start acting like an ant by contributing and conforming to society. God bless her soul, I know she means well.

My inner-conversation break-through occurred back in mid-2000. I received a random phone call from an old buddy of mine that I met in college. He mentioned that his friend was a casting director for a new TV pilot and that the show wanted a fresh Asian-American face. The directors scheduled the audition for that afternoon, so I cleared my schedule and immediately drove out to Hollywood.

On my way there, I felt confident. When I got there, I entered through the doors and moved down the hall to a waiting area that hosted another hopeful auditioner. As I approached the seating area, I said, "Excuse me, is this where the audition is?" She looked up, smiled, and said, "Yes." Oh my God! The woman was Bai Ling! Bai Ling is a Chinese-American actress who garnered success and fame during the mid-90's through the 2000's. She starred in movies like *The Crow*, *Wild Wild West* and *Crank: High*

Voltage. In 1998, *People* magazine listed her as one of the "50 Most Beautiful People in the World." While her risqué style and eccentric personality compromised her public image, she was still a respectable figure in the motion picture industry. Somewhat star-struck, I sat down sitting shoulder to shoulder with the actress. A minute passed and the door opened; Ling got up, looked back at me, and wished me luck.

I uncontrollably shivered as I rocked back and forth, rubbing both of my sweaty hands across my legs. I needed to gather my thoughts, so I got up and walked to the window. Talking to myself, I said, "God I'm such an idiot for coming! What was I thinking coming here to audition? This is the real deal for real actors, and I'm a freaking joke." My fear and panic mutated into blame and fury. I started blaming my friend for referring me to this opportunity. I was like, "How can this guy put me in such a situation like this and deliberately set me up for an embarrassing failure? I'm going to chew him out when I get out of here!" At this point, Bai Ling began her audition, so she started rehearsing a chaotic and demonstrative scene. I could hear the entire audition as if it were directly in front of me. I envisioned her convincing antics, facial expressions, and body language and thought, "I have to go next?"

Mike Tyson said that everybody has a plan until they get punched in the face. My face got caved in. I immediately headed for the door and walked back downstairs, frantically pacing around the foyer. Running out of things to do, I took the sign-in sheet and began to rummage through the listed names. A few names below mine, I recognized a familiar name: Aaron Takahashi. Aaron managed the local supermarket that I worked for as a stock boy. We used to crack each other up with our "old grandpa" impersonations. If a new shipment came in, I would get on the store's intercom and yell, "Aaron, new shipment, back dock!" in an old 85-year old, grandpa voice. A minute later, we'd meet up at the shipping dock and start laughing hysterically that nobody in the store caught on to our joke. I guess they just figured some old grandpa made the announcement. He always told me that he dreamed of becoming an actor. Today, Aaron has been featured in over 50 national commercials and is easily recognized as the "hilariously-nerdy Asian dude" on TV.

When I saw Aaron's name on that sheet, my inner voices became more constructive. I thought to myself, "If Aaron is out here in Hollywood doing this, then why can't I?" What do I have to lose by taking a crack at this opportunity? Back with Modus Dei, I performed in front of sold-out crowds and won them over. Who cares if I suck at acting? I'm going to go in and slap that director with my energy and swagger. The truth started taking over. I headed back up the stairs and sat on my chair as Bai Ling walked out and smiled once again. It was just another day for her.

The young casting director invited me in and placed me directly in front of a camera. She quickly introduced herself and debriefed my role as playing opposite to the star, Luenell, an African-American comedian, and actress. I had no time to let that sink in. I was on, "Hi, my name is Cary Hokama and I'm from Los Angeles, CA.".

I played the role of a grumpy Asian restaurant owner that significantly contrasted Luenell's role. Each time I read, I used a different Asian accent: The first was Japanese, the second was Chinese, and the third was a Korean accent. My cousin Marc and I grew up mimicking other Asian accents, so I totally killed the impersonation. The casting director laughed emphatically the whole time.

As I drove back, I couldn't help but feel like a million bucks. I began to believe that they would actually consider me for the role. The next day, my friend called me back with the news. "Cary, they said you were awesome and funny as f**k but unfortunately, you were a bit too raw and inexperienced." You know what? I was cool with that. I felt accomplished just by stepping out of my comfort zone and attempting something new and risky.

This one experience forever altered my understanding of who or what is in control of my inner conversations. If I ever doubt something or come across a fear-induced dilemma, I always go back to this experience. That day served as a reminder to fight off all the lies and act in according to the truth. Today, I'm still constantly discovering new voices, and it's exciting! For the negative ones, I've learned instantly to detect and destroy them. It's an incredible exercise to employ, and I challenge every one of you to practice and master this skill every single day.

If you went a long time without a guiding voice and finally found it—you're empowered. That's fantastic! Now, let's take it to the next level.

4TH COMPONENT: PARTICIPATION & COMMITMENT

"The distance between dreams and reality is called action."
—Unknown

We live in a culture that worships understanding. We settle for learning but don't act upon it. People crave insight. According to Hendre, insight is a drug. When you gain insight, your brain releases dopamine, and this tricks the body into thinking you have transformed. Back in the 80's and 90's, content reigned supreme, so everything focused on information. Think of the proverb *knowledge equals power*. While content may be relevant, context is everything. People misconstrued content for results and forgot about the essential elements required for breaking through. People strategize their development based on their needs, rather than implementing environmental requirements. I can explain this in so many ways, but ultimately, information without formation creates a mirage of transformation. The formulas for transformation looks like this:

Before:

Information = Transformation
Content = Results

Today:

Information + Formation = Transformation
Content + Context = Results
Participation = value.

Thank you Hendre ☺

As a Transformation Specialist, I create result-driven environments. Results happen when you engage and participate in your responsibilities. You cannot conclude something just because you understand it. It's not what you know that counts, it's what you do that matters most. In the end, all that matters is what you do. Nike's slogan, *Just Do It*, reflects life's greatest truth. Become a master of doing! When my time is up, I want my family and God to say, "Cary did it. He's done."

When you commit to a transformation, that decision reemerges more than once. From now on, every decision you make will either get you closer or further from your goals. If your goal is to have the best physique possible by your next birthday, then every decision you make from now will determine that outcome. How you spend your day, what foods you eat, and who you surround yourself with all influence this result. Your daily participation towards the final outcome dictates how successful or not you will be.

It sounds hardcore but it's the truth. Every minute of every day will either get you closer or further from your goal. If you feel lazy or uninspired to do something, remember that as each day passes you get that much closer to death. You have to make each day count. Remember that!

We can analyze our behaviors to see how they influence our present results. I'm not asking how busy you are. I'm busy. We're all super busy. Whenever people repeatedly mention that they're busy, it shows a lack of commitment. Furthermore, it's straight BS. Right now, think of a number between 1-10. Write it down so you can see the number physically as well. Where do you lie on that scale regarding your results? If you didn't choose a number, or already continued reading without thinking about this, I'm sorry, but you're automatically a 2. How do you feel about this number? Notice the internal conversations that surface when you see this number. Are you starting to hear your inner voices?

Are they starting to take over? Are you feeling a bit defensive? I'm going to be real with you. You may not like this, but this number reveals your level of participation and commitment in life. Some people commit themselves to reading and studying about personal transformations, yet they choose not to perform the actions they learn. There is nothing wrong with that. You can continue to read, listen, and study, but this time, get the results. We enable others by being nice and saving face, but remember tension can be healthy. Tension creates an opportunity for improvement because anything we can reveal, we can transform. What's it going to take for you to finally produce results?

What will you do differently with the new skill you are learning? How will you engage your staff or co-workers differently? How about when you spend time with your family? How about with your friends, your community, or your sphere of influence? See, if you take the information in but don't utilize it, you'll always be missing out. Participation creates an insight that differs from observation.

We see these types of people every day. The ones that go through the motions of day-to-day life without giving themselves. You can draw attention to yourself by making everything about you or by completely checking out. Whichever method you choose, you remain the special one. Whether you're loud and noticeable, or out and hiding, you focus on yourself and fail to create new experiences for yourself and those who surround you. The most powerful insight comes from creating value for others.

Do you know how many new things I discover while teaching? I continually learn as I teach and coach. Sometimes I say something cool, e.g., I'll reframe an action using metaphors, and I think to myself, "Wow that was pretty amazing." There is value in creating value; it's kind of like karma—right? If you isolate yourself, you attract attention, but you also miss the opportunity associated with creating value for others.

Whether it's at work, school, church, or within your circle of family and friends, you will always encounter the obnoxious guy or girl. Just because they're loud does not mean that they are giving. Other people suffer when you don't participate because you withhold the value of sharing your sacred journey. You lie to yourself and believe that your disregard has no effect on others. They think, "It doesn't matter I can't attain my full potential because nobody needs me." That's a lie. People are waiting for your half of the commitment. There are some people that only you can influence. Only you. When you take a step into your future, you allow others to see it as well.

Going back to our 1-10 scale, if you stay at level 4 when you can advance to level 5, you set the standard for level 4, and your sphere of influence will consist of level 3's or below. Anybody above a level 4 will look for something better. You'll say, "Don't ask me anything, I'm at a 4 right now" or, "don't mess with me because you don't know what I've been through, and I have great reasons to stay at 4." However, when you break that mentality and bulldoze yourself to the next level, you allow others to do the same. Remember, living your life to its full potential is the greatest gift you can give to your loved ones.

Participate in your commitment and don't be afraid of showing the real you. People will make stuff up about you anyway, so it's up to you to show them what you're about. Participation plus commitment equals value.

5TH COMPONENT: LAW OF ATTRACTION

"In order to attract success in life, be attractive."
— Jim Rohn

Jim Rohn said, "In order to attract success in life, you need to be attractive." I LOVE THAT. In fact, I love that statement so much that I created my version of it: "I attract the greatest things in life by being greatly attractive." My friends, I'm not talking about physical or external attraction. We don't have to become Channing Tatum, *Magic Mike: XXL*. I'm talking about attraction from deep within. Over time, your inner world becomes your outer world and how you do anything, is how you do everything. My mind is my greatest destination, and its beauty and intricacy captivates me more than the Seven Wonders of the World. I honestly believe that.

As a kingmaker, I am willing to be misunderstood by others so that I can actualize my dreams. I don't worry about sharing my aspirations because not too many people have the drive needed to become successful. You become whoever you surround yourself with. They say that your salary reflects the average total income of the five people you spend the most time with. Eric Thomas, one of the most world-renowned motivational speakers, revealed whether he agreed with these statements or not. His response was, "I absolutely agree with it and that's why I hang out alone." My friend Six Reasons, a rapper who made it out of the tough streets of Watts, CA, always used to say, "Eagles don't fly with seagulls!"

Your mind and spirit possess infinite power. My inspiration and hero, Bruce Lee, said, "As you think, so shall you become." Biblical Proverb 23:7 says, "As a man thinks, so is he." Your mind is active, and it is palpable. Every day, I exercise my mind by syncing my thoughts with my spirit. What you think about all day is what you become.

When you embrace your dominant thoughts and set your goals, your actions will follow suit. Earl Nightingale said that when you set your goals, "Do not worry about how you will get there. Leave that up to a greater power than yourself. But if you know where you're going, the answers will come to you of their own accord." Asking how the Law of Attraction works parallels asking how being in love works. You can't explain that kind of love, right? Love is something dynamic; it constantly moves and expresses itself differently. It's an inexplicable emotion—a feeling. Whatever it is, you know it works, you know it exists, and you know it's real.

Like everything else, mastering the Law of Attraction begins and ends with you. You must change yourself before you can change your world. When you change, everything around you starts to change. Life should not center on what you can get, but rather on who you are and what you can give. That's the secret.

When I was the lead singer for Modus Dei, we primarily played at local coffee shops, bars, and even churches. One night, my band mate and I went to Hollywood's House of Blues to watch a rapper, Common, perform. The House of Blues is like the Mecca of music venues, and Common brought the house down that night. As we exited the show, I said to myself, "I guarantee, we will perform here one day." A year later, we not only played at the House of Blues but got reinvited to play at the House of Blues in Downtown Disney, adjacent to Disneyland.

It was 2003 and my buddy and I worked at a used bookstore owned by his parents. His parents would often stop by to check up on us and drop off some lunch. Due to their real estate investments, both of his parents retired and lived comfortably. One day during lunch, my buddy and his parents began openly discussing their real estate business in front of me. In a delicate and enthusiastic tone, I asked his parents the net worth of their real estate business and the mother said $11 million. Right then and there, I knew I had to get involved in real estate. I wanted to invest in properties so that I could build a passive income stream.

Several years after my music career ended, I launched a fitness business with a friend of mine. He had just received his real estate license and was looking to work for a brokerage company. I happened to have another friend who was a broker, so I introduced the two. The three of us got together for lunch and as those two discussed the tools of the trade, I began to think about real estate again. I thought about my friend's family who now owned more than 500 units all throughout Southern California and Hawaii. As my heart began to race, my broker buddy Abe, turned to me and said, "By the way Cary, you already have a green light if you want to get into real estate. I will help you get set up and teach you everything you need to know." I knew I was going to get involved and that statement confirmed it.

Later that week, I met Abe at his new office so that we can discuss our plan. When we sat alone, our conversation had very little do with the real estate business itself. He knew that I had recently launched my fitness and coaching business, and I knew that he had signed a huge lease for a new corporate office. We began talking about our journey, our personal lives, my marriage, his relationship, our past failures and mistakes in business, as well as our significant accomplishments in life.

I thanked him for giving me the opportunity to get into real estate. His benevolence gave me a chance to fulfill one of my lifelong goals. I openly and honestly told Abe why I chose to pursue the business. I did not intend on becoming the top producing real estate agent at his brokerage. Instead, I hoped to become a real estate investor, just like my friend's parents. I wanted to purchase and broker my first multi-unit deal with my wife and my mother.

I told him that I ultimately wanted to travel the world—with my wife—as an international speaker, author, and life coach. I envisioned myself making a huge impact in the office by positively influencing other agents. Making accomplishments with a friend amplifies the rewards. We tackle obstacles together, hold each other accountable, and enjoy the gifts of our success. We promised each other that after my first multi-unit purchase, we would travel to Italy as a celebration. We shook hands, gave each other a hug, and that was that. Four months later, I got my real estate license and joined Landmark Real Estate.

In April of 2015, I entered escrow for a multi-unit property. Aileen, my mother, and I spent a year and a half searching for the perfect property. During that time, we checked out over a hundred duplexes in the Los Angeles area and at one point even considered giving up on the game plan. We complicated the search by obsessing over our criteria, budget, and location. When this particular duplex came on the market, I immediately went to take a look at it.

The listing agent was assembling the property's *for sale* sign as I arrived. He invited me inside and told me that he would tour the property as soon as he finished putting up the sign. As I entered and began touring the interior, I noticed that the house fit all our outlined criteria. As we walked the property, the seller of the home, an old Korean man, popped out of the master bedroom and greeted me with a warm welcome. I was surprised that the owner was present because that's usually not the case during an open house.

I felt the Law of Attraction at work. The open house ended, and the listing agent left, but Mr. Choi and I kept talking for the next two hours. He gave me a complete tour of the duplex and walked me around the neighborhood. After some time, Mr. Choi's wife came home, and he introduced me to her. I introduced myself and told her that my wife Aileen, is also Korean. A few days later, I brought my mom and Aileen over to the house, but unfortunately, the realtor had not scheduled another open house. We walked up to the duplex as if the Choi's invited us over as guests. After some scrutiny, my mother and Aileen discovered that the duplex presented a unique situation that combined value and opportunity. I realized that if we made the right offer, the Choi's would favor us as potential buyers. We thanked them for their time and generosity and left to prepare the offer.

Within the offer package, I inserted a photo of our beautiful family from a trip we took to Northern California. Also, I presented a cover letter that captured our love and excitement for the property and neighborhood. I explained that my wife and I sought a duplex so that we can live attentively close to my aging mother. Apparently, our offer aligned with their exact asking price. A few days later, the listing agent called and congratulated us on opening escrow. He revealed that the Choi's received several other offers, but chose ours due to our compatibility. The escrow process requires patience and diligence because many contingencies and procedures threaten the escrow's end. I won't get into details, but I specifically knew that the loan process would define whether we bought this property or not. For the next 30 days, I changed things around. I drove by the duplex every day and envisioned myself living there. I even had to duck a few times so that Mr. Choi didn't see me regularly drive by.

Between loan complications and a lingering escrow, Mr. Choi began to grow impatient. Regardless, I still drove to the duplex every day and even started using it as a daily starting point. For example, if I wanted to go to the gym, I would go to the duplex first and envision myself leaving the house. I established the route from the duplex as my new standard. Even after the gym, I would first drive to the property before heading back to my current house. After some time, I focused on assimilating myself into the duplex's neighborhood: I shopped at the nearby grocery stores, visited the local coffee shops, and ate at the surrounding restaurants. Everything I did revolved around living in the new duplex. At times I felt foolish; however, I knew that utilizing the Law of Attraction increased the likelihood of closing escrow.

Brokering my deal turned the purchase into a fairy tale. Not only did I purchase my first multi-unit property, but I also received a nice commission check from Abe. Over three years had passed since Abe and I shook hands in his office and since that time, we have traveled together to Las

Vegas, San Francisco, Napa, Lanai, Maui, Spain, and of course, Italy! Abe and I even partnered on other businesses and non-profit ventures. In 2015, Landmark Real Estate awarded me as their *Most Inspirational Leader*.

The Law of Attraction does not fixate on outcomes. I know it seems counter-intuitive, but the exercise concentrates on who you are and what you give out. The attraction begins from inside, and the rest follows when you surrender the outcome to a greater power. I have no other explanation for this phenomena because this 5th component works only when you do. You must exercise this ability daily and incorporate it into your lifestyle. Now I'm going to elaborate on the Law of Attraction's most essential, result-oriented actions.

1. Start your day early and avoid the chatter of everyday life! Whatever you do within the first thirty minutes of waking up dictates the tone for the rest of the day. I'd highly suggest the book, *Miracle Morning* by Hal Elrod. It changed my life and helped thousands of others as well. I used to hate mornings; after all, I was a rock star, right? I would go to bed at 4 A.M. and get up around 11 A.M. or noon. Now, waking up at 4 A.M. excites me. I train with my first set of clients at 6 A.M. and they, along with other trainers and their customers, always say, "Cary, how are you so happy and jolly this early in the morning?" I always respond, "It's easy because I get to wake up early to come and hang out

with you guys!" The truth behind my happiness lies in my morning routine. As I mentioned before, I wake up to reflect on the things I appreciate in life. I celebrate life through the use of powerful affirmations, prayer, and meditation. Even during my forty minute drive to the gym, I listen to leading thought leaders such as Tony Robbins, Les Brown, and Jim Rohn. Every morning I experience a taste of divinity. I deposit all of this happiness without having to interact with anyone: no emails, no Facebook, no Instagram, no distractions. This daily process carves out my personality for the day. I tell my client's that this routine allows me to be the active and confident coach they need me to be. Now, I don't expect everyone to get up at 4 A.M. as I do. For beginners, I recommend waking up an hour before your regular schedule. Once you arise, it's imperative to ignore your phone, emails, Instagram, Facebook, and even the stock market. I enable my phone's "Do Not Disturb" button from 9 P.M. to 5:15 A.M. On the days where I don't have clients, I usually wake up between 6 and 7 A.M. and immediately repeat the same cycle.

2. Each morning, do your 10-10-10's.
   - Write down 10 things you're grateful for
   - Write down 10 Affirmations
   - Do a quick daily devotional. Pray or meditate for 10 minutes.

Writing down 10 things you're grateful for:

This is such an incredible and empowering exercise. You MUST write down the things you are thankful for; you can't just think about it or say it out loud. I recommend purchasing one of those old school Composition Notebooks for this exercise—it helps keep things uniform. When I first started doing this, my list consisted of 10 simple things that looked something like this:

10 Things I'm grateful for:

1. Aileen (my wife)
2. Mom
3. Dad
4. Marcy (sister)
5. House
6. My Job
7. My Car
8. Books
9. The Gym
10. My Health

You get the idea.

Four years have passed since I started doing this exercise. This practice challenges me to think deep and in-depth so that I can demonstrate a higher level of appreciation. Even the biggest pessimist can harbor optimism by acknowledging their gratitude. Currently, my list has evolved into something like this:

10 Things I'm grateful for:

1. Aileen - For always having such a pleasant attitude and for encouraging me to pursue my goals no matter what it took.
2. Parents - For being the best example of hard work, discipline, and sacrifice. They sacrificed everything to raise my sister and me.
3. Marcy - For always believing that I was special and that I'd do something extraordinary with my life.
4. My House – I own the perfect house. I have my own office and enjoy the beautiful weather of Southern California.
5. My Business - I am truly grateful for my clients and my career. I facilitate transformations and help people progress through a priceless journey
6. Health – I'm in the greatest shape of my life. I take care of my body through exercise, healthy eating, and Jiu-Jitsu training with Aileen.

You get the idea.

Next, write down 10 Affirmations. When you do this exercise, do not write down words and move on to the next line. Let the affirmation soak into your mind as you implement its meaning. Ask yourself, "Why, am I thinking of these qualities and statements? What makes you be about what you're affirming instead of talking about it?" For example:

10 Affirmations:

1. I am mentally tough and unstoppable
2. I am made perfect by my Creator
3. I am a servant leader
4. My passion shows up every day and is undeniable to others
5. I am full of positive energy and action
6. I am committed to the mastery of my craft
7. I am legacy-minded; my spirit will live on forever
8. I am a committed and devoted husband to Aileen
9. Confidence and courage overtake my fears
10. I am a kingmaker

Again, writing down an affirmation does not suffice. As you have noticed by now, you have to align these statements with your entire being. You have to find intent and know exactly why you chose to affirm these qualities. Joel Osteen released a powerful video on YouTube called the *Power of I Am*. If you can, please check it out for yourself. He explains that whatever you say about yourself, whether negative or positive, will affect you. Do not give negative forces the chance to invade your mind. Trust me;

your external surroundings will fabricate enough negativity—no need to create more.

The last of the 10-10-10's consists of daily devotional prayer or meditation for 10 minutes. Feel free to modify this exercise along your own beliefs and spirituality. I use the website *My Utmost For His Highest* as a resource for my daily devotional. Sometimes I use an iPhone app called *Self-Help Classics*. The app includes a collection of thirty personal development books that you can read for free. As you learn, take down notes that highlight the main focus of the content. I usually spend five minutes writing down compelling quotes, sentences, or paragraphs. Following my read, I spend five minutes praying, meditating, or even stretching on a foam roller. Regardless of the activity, I dedicate those five minutes to deep thinking. If you don't know how to meditate, I recommend reading *Success Through Stillness* by Russell Simmons. It will change the way you think about meditation.

Again, you can modify this exercise accordingly. Just don't amend it in a way that accommodates your comfort zone. The whole challenge of this exercise starts by choosing something different and challenging. We produce different results by stimulating novel thoughts.

I've partitioned my garage into a personal office, jiu-jitsu dojo, and personal sanctuary. Before I begin my 10-10-10's, I turn off the garage's clinical lights and, instead, light 2-3 candles. I augment the setting with ambient music that I find on YouTube. While doing this exercise, I prefer to digest lyric-less music because words distract you from your thought process. The point is for you to sync your mind and spirit harmoniously.

I have practiced this routine for almost four years. This daily ritual facilitated the biggest change in my life. I thank Hal Elrod and his book for challenging me to create a morning miracle system. I randomly look back at some of the stuff I wrote down from 2012, and it is just mind-boggling. I jotted down things that I don't even remember writing down; however, reading those old statements affirms my growth, and my accomplishments throughout this journey. You realize that your life did not progress via miracles or coincidence, but rather through thoughts and affirmations. Do the work, do your 10-10-10's, and watch as you become unstoppable. Now that we've covered the mind we must balance the equation by incorporating your body.

Chapter 2
Step 2: Nutrition - Master your food

"Nutrition isn't just about eating, it's learning how to live."
— Patricia Comptton

Before I begin, I know that the topic of food and nutrition can galvanize many of you. Many people refuse to compromise individual food choices regardless of their health aspirations. I implore you to keep an open mind and not to skip this section. As a food enthusiast myself, I understand that food intersects across community, family, life, and culture.

Although I am a Certified Holistic Nutritionist, I cannot, nor care to, scientifically prove the information within this chapter; I don't plan on authoring a science textbook. The principles I share come from a blend of dedicated learning and personal experimentation. I adjusted these concepts in light of my personal transformation and tweaked some ideas based on successes and failures. With that said, I am hungrier than ever to study the human body. Understanding this complex mechanism fuels my obsession to learn; I hope it does for you as well. How we fuel our body dictates how we look and feel. Our body represents an actual figure of our dietary behavior and how you look, usually determines the kind of life you live.

Many years ago, I remembered telling my buddy that I wanted to get my first tattoo. He strongly opposed my idea and began lecturing me on The Bible and its emphasis on treating our bodies like sacred temples.

He weighed 70-80 pounds over normal, so I kept rolling my eyes at his hypocrisy. I thought to myself, man, this guy needs to fix his perspective. I don't like to use the word wrong, but what's your perspective of a healthy body?

In the beginning, my nutritional perspective lied somewhere between Charles Barkley and Al Bundy. I devoured fast-food and sat on my ass as I gained forty pounds while working for Fox Sports. I knew I had to change things, so I decided to address my eating habits first. I made a vow not to stop at KFC or Papa John's on the way to work, and I also told myself that I would no longer buy the cheeseburger, fries, and Coke combo for lunch. My diet included a lot of fast food so what did I do instead? I went to Trader Joe's. I thought that purchasing any food from Trader Joe's made for a healthy alternative. I felt good about buying instant Kung Pao Noodles, a box of red licorice, and organic soda.

Over the years, a lack of physical results funneled me into trying every fad diet in existence: the Master Cleanse Lemonade Diet, the Paleo Diet, the Atkins Diet, the Cabbage Soup Diet, and the IIFYM Diet.

At one point, my buddy and I even tried *The Bulking Diet*—a diet that consisted of eating and drinking anything to gain weight and build large muscles. That was bad.

I've learned over the years that the perfect diet does not exist. Eating is like art; it's personal and unique. What works for one person may not work for another. You define your interpretation of health when you learn about wholesome foods and their effects on your body. They say your nutritional habits contributes to 80% of your physique, so you simply cannot outwork a bad diet. Your health is your true wealth. What does "keeping your body sacred" mean to you? How do you achieve real health and how important is it? Does your health get in the way of reaching some of your ultimate life goals? How much do you pay in monthly medical bills and how often do you take pills to mitigate symptoms? Does your health problem affect any relationships in your life? People put premium gas in their expensive cars and then drive to McDonald's for lunch. Does this make sense to you?

As a holistic nutritionist, certified by NCEP, I've not only received an extensive formal education on nutrition, but I've also implemented a stable 5-component nutrition system that I successfully use myself. While I no longer practice as a nutritionist, I believe that the method I created for myself will help transform your overall health and wellness. Using this system, you can consistently maintain a healthy and lean body year round. You don't have to obsess when it comes to eating properly. It is ultimately up to you to make conscious decisions regarding the direction of your health. My goal here is to educate you more and help you get on the right track so that you can create a lasting and nourishing lifestyle.

1st Component: Know your pH balance

When you purchase a used car—despite what the exterior looks like—the first place you scrutinize is under the hood, right? Of course! You want to know how the car runs! Running a diagnostic test at the mechanic lets you know what parts need to be fixed or improved. Knowing your pH balance acts as a physical diagnostic test.

Bear with me now as most of the following scientific explanations have been taken directly out of the NCEP text book. The term pH stands for potential of hydrogen. It calculates the amount of hydrogen ions in a particular solution. As the acidity of that solution increases so does the concentration of hydrogen ions. When hydrogen ions decrease, the solution becomes more alkaline.

People measure pH on a scale of 0 to 14, and the number 7 imparts a neutral pH. The human body possesses a slightly alkaline pH, as blood pH levels range from 7.35 to 7.45. Bicarbonates keep our body at a nearly neutral level through a process known as homeostasis. The lower the pH, the more acidic your body is, and the higher the number, the more alkaline. It's important to know that most foods have a naturally alkaline pH; however, manufacturing processes often make these foods acidic. To maintain your health, I recommend that meals consist of a 75% alkaline to 25% acidic balance. Further, your dietary intake should naturally balance your body pH.

You can purchase pH test strips online or at your local drug store and can use these saliva strips to test your pH balance level at home. Your goal is to be as close to 7.4 as possible. Once you know your level, you can recalibrate your nutrition so that you fall into the 7.35 - 7.45 range. Keep in mind that your level of activity throughout the day, as well as your level of stress, can affect your pH balance. Think of your pH challenge as a food chess match. You don't have to check your pH balance every day but once a month would be a great start!

2ND COMPONENT:
EAT 3-5 WELL-BALANCED MEALS A DAY CONSISTING OF WHOLE FOODS

Eat every 3.5-4 hours and eat 3-5 meals a day depending on the length and activity of your day. I average around four meals a day, which usually includes a whey protein shake. My goal is to maximize my athletic performance while making sure to stay lean and muscular year round. Eating multiple, well-balanced meals—consisting of whole foods—allows you to maintain a stable blood sugar level. This way of eating prevents fluctuations and provides a steady stream of energy throughout the day. Including protein at each of these meals allows a constant flow of amino acids to repair muscles and create hormones. These processes typically occur in the bloodstream and signal to the rest of the body that everything is all good and functioning as should be.

Organic vs Commercial

Personally, I do my best to eat organic foods; especially when it comes to certain meats, veggies, and fruits. I like to blend the fruits and veggies into a smoothie, occasionally using it as a meal replacement. After extensively researching the benefits of organic foods, eating commercialized and processed foods no longer made sense. In the end, I realize that the government can always manipulate studies to back up commercial farming, and vice versa.

Sadly, I believe that the food industry favors profit over health and wellness. These corporations will spend millions marketing their product in any way that can sway public perception. When it comes to your health, you are responsible for finding accurate and reliable information. Look at the facts, process the information, and utilize the things that make sense to you. Some of you may decide to cut red meat entirely from your diet. I know I had to think long and hard about my choices after seeing a few things; however, sticking to a carnivorous diet made the most sense for me. I just enjoy my steaks too much!

My grandmother on my mother's side lived the cleanest life possible. She never smoked or drank, and she never ate red meat, pork, or shellfish of any kind. Her meals mainly consisted of veggies and fish. Even though she maintained an unparalleled standard of health, she got breast cancer and suddenly died due to a heart attack in her early 70's. On the contrary, my grandfather on my father's side fulfilled the yin to my grandmother's yang. He always purchased food from the discount store and hardly ate any organic foods. To be honest, I don't think he even knows what organic food means. He was always gung-ho about the cheap stuff! Not to mention, his primary source of water came from his kitchen faucet. Today, he's 92 years old and still strong as an ox.

The fate of my grandparents always messed with my head. When I'm at the store comparing prices of organic versus non-organic foods, I always think, "Is this really going to matter? Am I wasting my money paying top dollar for organic foods?" Research from the early 1900's implicates that, back then, only 1 out of 4000 Americans got cancer. Today, 1 out of 2 people will get some cancer by the end of their lives. That is staggering. America suffers from the highest obesity rates in the world. Whether you're in Asia or Europe, you can spot an American from a mile away. In the end, I believe that health begins with knowing what you put into your body, so try eating foods that mitigate your chances of contracting today's deadliest diseases.

So here's my guide to eating through a practical, 3-5 meal-per-day system. First off, try your best to eat every 4 hours. I eat every 4 hours so that my body can fully digest the food. When you do eat, eat to only 80% of your maximum capacity. It's a bit hard to explain what 80% full feels like because it's your body and only you can feel it. For me, that feeling surfaces when I satisfy my hunger. At that point, I know I can still eat more, but also, can go out and be active if I wanted to. Since I do live a very active lifestyle, I try to eat enough food so that I can work out or do Jiu-Jitsu in the next 30 minutes. Back in the day, I used to eat until I could barely walk. I was *that guy* who inflated his stomach to the point of no return. Often, I would sit on the couch and unzip my pants just so that I can breathe. Many times, I overate out of courtesy for the people preparing the food, but I no longer feel this way. It is my body, and I want to treat my body with the utmost respect and care.

I always find ways to include dark leafy greens and veggies as my main source of carbohydrates and fiber. When I do eat non-fruit or vegetable carbs, I stick with eating mainly complex carbs (whole grains, brown rice, beans, and nuts). The opposite of complex carbs are simple carbs (white rice, white bread, white pasta, etc.) Try your best to avoid these as these type of carbs metabolize into simple sugars, which we will get into next.

All of my meals incorporate some protein, 1 type of complex carb (try not to mix different carbs in a meal), and some source of healthy fats. For example, for breakfast, I'll eat 4-5 organic whole eggs (protein & fat), turkey bacon (protein), and two whole grain waffles (complex carb). Another meal may include a steak or chicken breast, some brown rice, and leafy greens topped with pine nuts or olive oil. Don't bother measuring your food portions unless you're competing in a physique or bikini competition. Instead, use your hands as a tool to proportionately measure each element of food—don't complicate your meals by measuring out, or logging everything. It's a silly way to live, don't you think? As I mentioned, leave measuring out macronutrients to the physique competitors.

3rd Component: Avoid Sugar, Sugar Substitutes, Refined / Processed Foods, and yes, Alcohol!

Researchers currently rank cocaine as the second most addictive substance to humans. Guess what number one is? Sugar! That's why manufacturers incorporate sugar into almost every food and liquid product on the market. For example, any ingredient that ends in "ose" is a sugar. Manufacturers even add sugar to things like cigarettes because of its addictive nature. Four hundred years ago, enriched sugar did not even exist. Today, the average American consumes approximately one-hundred and seventy pounds of sugar per year. That's equivalent to eating five car tires worth of sugar! Horrific. A doctor by the name of Candice Pert stated very strongly that consuming sugar does not differ from shooting heroine (heroine is sugar) into your body. I want you to realize that sugar is a drug, poison, and nonfood.

Dr. Refa explains in his book, *Body Wise*, that one tablespoon of sugar can suppress the immune system for up to four hours. Now think, the average teenager drinks three cans of soda a day. Each can contains an average of 10 tablespoons of sugar! Drinking more than one soda a day raises your risk of serious weight gain by 80%. It is pertinent to understand that our bodies cannot handle such large amounts of sugar on a regular basis. Consuming too much sugar can trigger headaches, tooth decay, and indigestion.

I spent most of my time writing this book at coffee shops. One day, as I sat in the coffee shop, I ordered the regular: a black coffee with no room for cream or sugar. This day, in particular, I craved something sweet. I took a few sips and realized that the coffee failed to satisfy my taste buds, so I went to the little station and all across I saw raw sugar, Equal, Splenda, or Sweet n Low. I don't consume artificial sweeteners, so I went over to the barista and asked for Stevia. The employee disclosed that the franchise does not carry Stevia, due to environmental implications. He told me that if a company as large as theirs provided stevia, commercialization would deplete the world of stevia plants. So this company would rather kill people than kill the plants that produce a naturally derived sweetener?

Avoid sugar substitutes like your mother-in-law. Dangerous man-made chemicals such as aspartame present serious health consequences. Despite the reduced sugar content, these toxins harm the body by causing irreversible cell damage. Furthermore, these sugar substitutes dehydrate your body, fooling your brain into craving more carbohydrate-based foods and liquids. Research shows that those who consume artificial sweeteners eat up to three times the number of calories as groups who don't use it. Some of the side effects of artificial sweetener use include seizures and even death.

Aspartame is 180 to 200 times sweeter than sugar. You can find aspartame in a variety of products; however, they are mostly utilized in diet sodas. Aspartame makes up for 80 to 85% of food complaints registered with the FDA. Despite these numbers, its use within a variety of products remains legal. Numerous independent studies in aspartame found dangerous side effects in rodents. Nevertheless, the FDA chose not to acknowledge these findings when it approved the sweetener for public use. Many of the carcinogenic side effects of aspartame are beginning to surface within humans. Unfortunately, consumer demand and profitability allows it to remain on store shelves.

I recommend using Stevia, a zero-calorie natural sweetener, above all other sugar substitutes.

Indigenous to South America, the leaves of the *Stevia rebaudiana* plant tastes 150 times sweeter than sugar. In fact, the indigenous population of South America chews them for their sweet taste and uses them to sweeten beverages naturally. (referenced: global stevia institute).

I had the hardest time omitting soda, ice cream, cookies, brownies, and sour gummy candies from my diet. As much as I enjoyed sweets, consuming all of that junk food damaged my body. Sometimes I'll enjoy a small frozen yogurt, but for the most part, I have completely cut out sweets, desserts, juices, and sodas from my diet. Interestingly, I no longer even crave those types of food. As a matter of fact, I cringe when I see adults eating unreasonable amounts of sugary foods and treats.

When I do crave something sweet, I'll either eat an apple, banana, raisins, or dates. Most of the time, I just need to satisfy my craving, so these foods do an excellent job of taking care of that. Avoid sugar as much as you can and you'll see tremendous results!

4TH COMPONENT: DRINK AT LEAST HALF YOUR BODY WEIGHT IN OUNCES OF WATER EVERY DAY!

I know you have probably heard this all of your life, but you truly have to drink plenty of water! There's an excellent saying that quotes, "You're not sick, you're thirsty." Water plays a pivotal role in almost all biological functions. Most people know the importance of water; however, they do not understand the significance of consuming the proper amount.

You should be aware that our bodies are made up of 75% water—or saltwater to be exact. To properly digest the foods we eat, we need to consume a certain amount of water with each of our meals. Our muscles, ligaments, and tendons also require plenty of water. Water keeps our muscles pliable, flushes out metabolic wastes, and helps deliver nutrients throughout the body. Our joints would suffer the most without H_2O. If the synovial cavities don't receive enough water, our joints become stiff and rigid. Also, our brain requires the greatest need for water. The brain functions through the use of electrical transmissions and since ionized water can act as an ideal electrical conductor, the saline solution within your cranium ensures that those electrical communications operate flawlessly.

Water makes up 90% of our blood and every four months our body builds new blood cells to replace the ones lost to apoptosis. Dehydration significantly hampers this process and makes regenerating blood cells extremely difficult. Knowing this, do you now feel like you give your body the proper amount it needs?

Here is a list of many diseases and ailments that are augmented when your body lacks water:

- High Blood Pressure & Hypertension (due to over-working kidney)
- Asthma
- Ulcers
- Allergies
- Arthritis
- Lower Back Pain
- Stress
- Alzheimer's Disease
- Poor Digestion
- Muscle Soreness
- Chronic Pain
- Dry Mouth

Dehydration contributes to all of the issues listed above. I hope that this list will promulgate your daily water consumption priorities!

My clients always tell me, "I drink plenty of water." Do you say this or hear people say the same thing? Do you know if you drink enough water? How much water should you drink? Do you include juices, coffee, and tea as part of your water intake? These questions arise from a combination of ignorance, mystery, and marketing.

Water consumption guidelines suggest that we need to drink eight glasses of water a day. That's roughly 64 ounces of water. That's great and all, but people have different lifestyles and needs; therefore, a general prescription of 64 ounces cannot apply to everyone. Recent studies suggest that to acquire minimum hydration, the human body needs to have half of its weight in ounces of water every day. Most people see this as too much, but remember, the amount scales ounces, not pounds. How much is half your body weight in ounces of water? Let's look at a couple of different people.

Male: 220lbs = 110 ounces of water; to give you a visual, a liter of water is 32oz of water.

Female: 140lbs = 70 ounces of water

Now let's go back to the general water consumption guideline. If the male drank 64 ounces of water every day, he would undermine his need by 46 ounces! That is almost a liter and a half! When you begin to scale this deficit daily, monthly, and yearly, it becomes evident that the male's bound for dehydration destruction. Applying the same principle to the female, she still experiences a 6 ounce deficit. While her deficit is not as extreme as the males, over time, she will begin to experience the minor effects of dehydration.

Certain foods and beverages can escalate the effects of dehydration. Anything carbonated, sweetened, caffeinated, and especially artificially sweetened will assist in speeding up dehydration. Juice is not water, coffee is not water, and a Diet Coke certainly is not water. For you coffee lovers out there, they say that you lose approximately a cup and a half of water when you drink a cup of coffee.

No substitute exists for clean and fresh water. Water sources and purification techniques can vary; therefore, we must be cautious of how we get our water. The debate on consuming tap water has raged on for more than twenty years. Most tap water contains chlorine, algaecides, oxidants, pH inhibitors, fluoride, and lead. Some cities have cleaner and safer water supplies; therefore, I highly recommend researching your town's water supply. Some people install reverse osmosis water filters in their homes. These systems remove the greatest amount of water impurities and provide the cleanest and healthiest water possible. Unfortunately, this method can be a bit costly and unreasonable to some people, so cheaper methods do exist. Companies such as Pur and Brita provide accessible water filtering systems that you keep in your fridge and buying bottled water presents another option. Many recommend drinking artesian, but again, in the end, you are responsible for finding accurate and reliable information. Look at the facts, process the information, and tailor the facts to your lifestyle and budget.

Alcohol. Consuming alcohol frustrates our body's design. When children first try a sip of beer or vodka, the immediate response is, "Yuk!" Alcohol metabolizes into the simplest and purest form of sugar. Once it reaches the stomach, the alcohol absorbs through the stomach lining, entering directly into the bloodstream. Wine coolers and mixed drinks consist of a combination of sugars, so consuming these drinks can cause a severe blood sugar crash that damages the stomach lining. Although I've grown to appreciate certain red wines and beers, I've almost completely cut alcohol out of my life as well. The consequences of consuming liquor outweigh the fun and taste of consuming it.

Honestly, fulfilling your minimum daily water intake is not that difficult. Many stores sell stainless steel or high-quality BPA free water bottles that you can carry around all day. Throughout the day, I take a twenty-four-ounce stainless steel flask that lets me gauge my water intake. I know that I need to drink at least three bottles full to reach my minimum requirement; this simplifies things considerably. On regular days, where I wake at 4 A.M. and go to bed at 10 P.M., I purchase a gallon of water on the way to see my clients, and I drink the water from this jug to ensure proper hydration. I approach my water intake as a game or challenge. I know this may be TMI (too much information) for some of you, but make it a personal goal to see colorless urine. When you start to see some yellow, you know that you need to step your water game up.

Remember biological functions require water; therefore, water should be the corner stone to everyone's health. When evaluating your health, pay close attention to your water consumption because the amount of water consumed, or lack of will give you a great picture of your total health.

5TH COMPONENT: PROPER SUPPLEMENTATION

The subject of nutrition cannot be complete without addressing the importance of proper supplementation. Just to be clear, I'm not talking about performance supplements such as creatine, nitric oxide, BCAAs, glutamine, etc. I'm talking about the supplements needed for overall holistic health. Supplements provide the missing components from your whole food nutrition. No matter how good you think you eat, your diet usually consists of some deficiencies as many foods may not have every nutrient that you need. For this reason, I believe that the following supplements should construct the platform of any other supplements you take. The five supplemental recommendations for a healthy life are:

1. High Fiber

At the time of his death, Elvis Presley had more than forty pounds of fecal matter (yes, poop) within his intestinal tract; John Wayne had more than fifty pounds. That's disgusting and unacceptable my friends. During the early 1900's, the American diet consisted of 40% fibrous vegetables paired with nuts and certain grains. Nowadays, the most fiber an average American teenager will get comes from a slice of wilted lettuce in their hamburger.

Fiber plays a significant role in diet and general health. This indigestible material scrapes product and waste through the intestinal tract. Let's look at something real quick. A drainless or stagnant pond grows moss and algae, and the shaded or warmer areas build particular yeast or bacteria. When you catch a whiff, how does that pond smell? It smells like wet crap—right? The only living things you come across are mosquitoes and other parasitic insects. This same principle carries over to your intestinal tract. When you don't consume enough fiber, waste products flood your intestines, filling it with nasty and bacteria ridden rubbish.

Incorporating fiber into your diet is nearly effortless. Here's a list of some foods that are high in fiber:

- Carrots
- Apples
- Pear
- Celery
- Bananas
- Bell Peppers
- Prunes
- Dates
- Onions
- Spinach
- Nuts (avoid peanuts)

I made this short list just to show that almost every vegetable, and some fruit, has some fiber. Your dietary nuts (walnuts, raw almonds, cashews) possess a considerable amount of fiber, protein, carbohydrates, and nutritional oils as well.

If eating vegetables aren't your thing, juicing and blending provides a wonderful alternative. Believe the hype folks! For the past seven years, Aileen and I blend an amazing green smoothie daily. The smoothie consists of spinach, chard, kale, celery, lemon, apple, banana, and some ginger—all of which are organic. We blend first thing in the morning, cementing the practice as the cornerstone to our health. Consuming these greens does wonders for your body and skin tone while also providing the much-needed fibers within our diets.

You can easily Google different green smoothie recipes online; however, I want to emphasize the importance of a veggie dominant smoothie. Using too many fruits disturbs the balance of nutrients as fruits contain more sugars and calories than veggies.

In the evenings, my wife and I end our night with a fresh carrot, celery, and ginger juice. You can find organic carrots, celery, and most other veggies in large, inexpensive portions. Again, this may provide TMI but just like our little peeing game, do not be satisfied by pooping only once a day. Embrace the victory in pooping at least 2-3 times a day, if not more. It's one of the most satisfying and intrinsically rewarding feelings you will experience. Your body and your mind deserve it! You can think I'm crazy but give it a try and watch as you dramatically improve your life.

2. OMEGA 3's

This topic can get a little confusing so I'll do my best to break down an easier explanation. Research shows that the people of Okinawa, Japan live longer than any other group of individuals on Earth. Their diet mostly consists of fresh fish and plant-based foods. In 2015, I visited my ancestor's homeland and guess what foods I ate the most? Fish, shellfish, an assortment of sea kelp, vegetables, and rice. There exists two type of essential PUFA's (Polyunsaturated fatty acids): Omega-6 (linoleic acid) and Omega-3 (alpha-linolenic acid). When I say essential, I mean that our body cannot produce these nutrients on their own, therefore, we must obtain them through our diet. Americans consume a large amount of Omega-6 fats due to our large consumption of vegetable oils (e.g. corn, soybeans, safflower, sunflower, etc.). Unfortunately, we consume way too many Omega-6's and that influx harms our bodies.

We usually don't consume enough Omega-3s. Research suggests that we consume Omega-6 and Omega-3 fats in a 20:1- 50:1 ratio while the ideal ratio should be closer to 2:1 or even 1:1. When the ratio becomes this unproportionable, other mechanisms in the body give way to conditions such as Crohn's disease, increased rheumatoid arthritis, menstrual cramps, high blood pressure, strokes, and heart attacks. Omega-3's help guard against inflammation, blood clotting, constriction of blood vessels, and coronary heart diseases.

So what's practical? How can you achieve the proper Omega-6 to Omega-3 balance? Omega-3's come from wild-caught fish, seafood, and certain plant sources such as flaxseeds, chia seeds, and hemp seeds. Salmon, tuna, sardines, mackerel, and krill contain some of the most potent forms of omega-3 fatty acids. When eating organic, free-range eggs, be sure to eat the entire egg, as the yolk contains most of the beneficial fatty acids. I eat up to 6 whole eggs a day. Sometimes I eat them raw, mixing the eggs with some almond milk and a dash of cinnamon. Yum! A lot of people take fish oil supplements to balance their Omega-3 intake but unfortunately, only a few companies follow a strict standard of sourcing and manufacturing. In most cases, supplement companies take shortcuts so that they can maximize profits—just be aware of that. Do your research and buy the best quality fish oil pills if you choose to go that route.

Here's also what to include in your diet:

- High Quality Extra Virgin Olive Oil
- Coconut Oil
- Avocados
- Organic Grass-fed Butter
- Flaxseed Oil

What to avoid:

- Canola Oil
- Corn Oil
- Soy Oil
- Deep fried foods
- Commercial meat

3. Probiotics:

WebMD explains probiotics best: "Probiotics are live bacteria and yeasts that are good for your health, especially your digestive system. We usually think of bacteria as something that causes diseases. But your body is full of bacteria, both good and bad. Probiotics are often called "good" or "helpful" bacteria because they help keep your gut healthy." To further explain, our body possess live microorganisms called probiotics. These probiotics regulate 80% of our immune system. They help aid your digestive process, especially when it comes to constipation, gas, and diarrhea. Need I say more?

If probiotics live within our intestinal tract (our gut), and 80% of our immune system (a network of cells that keep your body healthy) comes from probiotics, how important is it to eat foods that replenish our probiotics? Without going into complex scientific detail, average Americans live with only half of the necessary probiotic value needed for normal health. That shouldn't surprise you. As we know, Americans suffer from the highest numbers of obesity and chronic diseases. Certain things such as heat, acid, antibiotics, and mineral imbalances destroy probiotics. Here's a list of foods that—when eaten in excess —can decrease your intestinal flora.

- Caffeine
- Sugar
- Milk/Dairy
- Meat
- Cooked Foods
- Alcohol
- Fried Foods
- Prescription Drugs

The foods we eat—and don't eat—influences the presence of probiotics within our bodies. These foods, when eaten in excess, can cause all sorts of problems. When you damage your intestinal flora, you damage your immune system, so how do we change this? Eating raw foods helps rebuild and improve our intestinal flora. The more raw food you can consume, the better. The fermented food contains a generous amount of bacteria that does all the fermenting! When we consume these bacteria, they act as the Miracle Grow or Chia Pet to our intestine. The probiotics grow stronger and more resistant to toxins and problem foods, strengthening the intestinal flora entirely.

Great sources of probiotics include:

- Organic Yogurt / Greek Yogurt (Avoid the sweetened ones with processed fruit)
- Organic Kefir
- Kombucha drink (Bottled drinks you can buy at most health food stores)
- Kimchi (Korean spicy pickled vegetables; mainly cabbage)
- Natto (Japanese fermented soybeans)
- Sauerkraut / Pickles

My mom is from Japan, so I've been fortunate enough to grow up eating natto and other Japanese dishes. Furthermore, since Aileen is Korean, her mom blesses us with a bulk delivery of homemade kimchi on a monthly basis. I understand that for many, eating natto and kimchi can be the grossest thing ever. I get it. The smell sucks compared to foods like pizza or pork chops, and the texture can be quite overwhelming. Kimchi, however, is more widely accepted due to the increasing popularity of Korean food. With that said, you now know the important role probiotics play in your system. You can also purchase supplemental probiotics that come in pill or tablet form. General guidelines suggest that you intake around 4-6 billion live cells daily. This number sounds a bit astronomical, but just know that each serving of probiotic tablets can provide up to 10 billion cultures.

Probiotic means *for life*. Can you eat too many probiotics? It's hard to say, but research suggests that you can't eat too many probiotics. For example, Koreans in general, eat kimchi in every meal but experts recommend using your body as a feedback system. If you experience painful and uncomfortable bowel movements, gas, constipation, or even bloating, then hold off on the probiotics for a bit and start building slowing again.

4. Enzymes

Today, the average American diet consists of more cooked foods than ever before. Few people eat raw foods; and because of this, we overwork our pancreas. Natural foods (even meats) possess enzymes that assist in breaking down nutrients.

Humans require enzymes for hundreds of different processes in the body. Enzymes help with hormone production, cellular energy, and the building and breaking down of tissues. Enzymes are the construction workers of your body: a lot of work, long hours, and little glamor. If you consistently use up your daily enzyme supply, how will your pancreas keep up with the demand? At first, your pancreas will work through it; however, if you allow this to become a habit, you will overwork and inflame your pancreas.

So here's a practical solution: start eating more raw foods and vegetables. Primary sources of digestive enzymes come from papayas, mangos, and pineapples. Eating some of the best tasting fruit in the world sounds like a treat if you ask me! With that said, you must consider the seasonality of the fruits and adjust them in your diet accordingly. If you choose not to consume those fruits, you can purchase digestive enzymes online or from your local health store. When buying a digestive enzyme supplement, make sure to read the label carefully and pay close attention to the sourcing. Some companies include synthesized enzymes in their products so be careful.

5. Multi-Vitamins

I don't want to sound like a broken record, but Multi-Vitamins are essential in providing micronutrients to your body. These micronutrients play a vital role in almost every function within your body. Like all of the supplements I've listed before, I encourage you to fulfill your vitamin intake via whole foods. Many health and online stores provide high-quality vitamin supplements in pill, tablet, or powder form. Feel free to use these, but don't rely on these manufactured vitamins as your primary source of micronutrients. Also, avoid multivitamins in gummy form. If you read the label, "gummies" almost always include sugar, glucose syrup, sucrose, and other forms of chemicals. Guys, these chemicals ultimately defeat the purpose of multivitamins! Purchasing an organic and natural *super greens* type of powder provides a convenient alternative. You can mix this powder with water and nearly receive the same benefits that stem from fruits and vegetables. Again, do your research and choose the best stuff out there.

Chapter 3
STEP 3: MASTER YOUR FITNESS & BODY

"Fitness is not a destination, it is a way of life."
—Unknown

When you think of the most successful and prolific personal trainer, whom do you think of? Some may say Jillian Michaels would fit the bill; she's beautiful, talented, fit, and famous. Others may say Tony Horton—the guy who created P90x—for developing his 90-day at-home DVD program that helped thousands of people get ripped. Others may say that today's CrossFit champions reign as fitness royalty due to the demanding nature of the sport. Lastly, others choose to epitomize the grandeur of fitness to whoever wins Mr. Olympia.

Nowadays with Facebook, Instagram, and other social media platforms, everybody and their moms consider themselves as some fitness celebrity, fitness coach, or online coach. I even came across a marketing scam that bundled fitness, nutrition, and life coaching certifications all in one. Yeah, it's gotten pretty bad. You can't upload a video of yourself working out and call yourself a trainer or a life coach!

Did you know that for the past 10+ years, Richard Simmons tops the list of global personal trainers? Yes, the old white dude with the fluffy hair who frolics around in a leotard! Sounds silly—right? But guess what? It's really not. He's actually the man! You see, being buff or shredded does not define fitness. Neither does "going beast mode" and impressing people at the gym all the time.

Richard Simmons could look into the eyes of unhealthy and morbidly obese women and men, and arouse a sense of hope. He allowed people to fall back in love with who they were, transforming fitness and presenting it as a way to love, embrace, and respect your body.

Simmons instilled such joy and hope in these women that they would dance with him on stage for the world to see. He created a global movement in the 80's and 90's. When you have a chance, look up Richard Simmons *Sweating to the Oldies* on YouTube; you will know what I'm talking about. Guys, you may chuckle and make fun at first, but that defines transformation. Let's see if any cocky meathead from the gym would be willing to do that! I seriously doubt it. So many misconceptions exist within the fitness community. At the end of the day, fitness augments personal development and assists in character building.

When it comes to physical mastery, your mind holds the reigns to a bodily transformation. Becoming physically fit stems as a byproduct of the journey you're on. Here are my 5 components to the mastery of body transformation:

1st Component: Resistance Training / Weight Training

Folks, the key to a stronger, more toned body comes from weight or resistance training. How you will train depends on the specificity of your goals. If you plan on looking like a bodybuilder or becoming one, I recommend working isolated muscle groups. For those that prioritize functionality, I recommend sticking to compound exercises that incorporate multi-joint movements. As a Certified Holistic Personal Trainer, I grasp the standards of the NCEP organization. I emphasize full body strength by building upon the seven primal movements. These movements are:

1. Squat (Back Squat, Goblet Squat, Air Squat, Front Squat, etc.)
2. Lunge (Walking Lunge, Split Lunge, Step-up, Side-lunge, etc.)
3. Push (Push-ups, Bench Press, Dumbbell Press, Shoulder Press, Incline Press, etc.)
4. Pull (Pull-Ups, Rows, Cable Face Pulls, DB rows, etc.)
5. Bend (Dead Lifts, Cleans, etc.)

6. Twist (Core Choppers, Dumbell Maison Twists, etc)
7. Gait (Walking, Lunging, Jumping, etc.)

This book won't go into the specifics of exercises and movements. This book guides you through a holistic transformation, not a workout routine. In regards to exercises and movements, a plethora of resources exist online that you can look up and research. With that said, I want to be very firm about the next topic. What is the ultimate secret to health and fitness that most people don't consider? Can you guess? The mind! Most people aren't aware of the connection between our mind and our muscles. You achieve maximum contraction when you consciously focus on each movement and each muscle group involved in an exercise—which is everything. People get way too caught up in how many sets they've done, or how many reps they put in, or how many days they went to the gym this week. That is not what's important.

When somebody proudly tells me that they spent three hours in the gym, I always ask, "Okay, but what did you do and how did you do it? How are you controlling your breathing patterns?" As I always profess, "everything begins and ends in the mind. And how you do anything is how you do everything." The best bodybuilders and fitness experts in the world all play a different game. They mentally dial in and connect to their craft on a holistic level. They even go as far as showing respect to the weights and equipment, gently caring for them and correctly placing them where they belong. Their work inside the gym applies to how they conduct their personal lives. That is the holistic approach to it.

2ND COMPONENT: CARDIOVASCULAR TRAINING - KNOW WHY YOU'RE DOING CARDIO!

Cardio, in my humble opinion, is by far the most misused and misconceived element in all of fitness. I studied sports medicine for the first three years of college and also served as a student-athlete trainer for one year. Even with all of this experience, I have trouble grasping the topic of cardio. Since 2009, I have trained clients from all walks of life, and over the years people seem to share consistencies with their language and thought process. I want to debunk this misconception right now. For so many years, whether directly through clients, friends or other people's conversations, people align cardio with weight loss and as a remedy to nutritionally related matters. For example, I frequently hear people say something like, "Damn, I ate crap all weekend. I need to run 10 miles!" Or, "I ate six slices of pizza! I'm going to the gym to do at least 3 hours of cardio!"

I had an old friend who told me he ran at least seven miles a day so that he can eat whatever he wants and not gain weight. Folks, when you talk this way or think this way, you erroneously use cardio. In the long run, this mentality can be dangerous. We must establish proper focus moving forward. First off, cardiovascular training strengthens your heart and builds endurance; this defines the purpose of cardio. We do need endurance and a healthy heart to improve our overall quality of life; however, you simply cannot outwork a bad diet. You must combat bad foods with healthy foods and attack a poor lifestyle with a good way of life. It's like knowingly upsetting your wife or husband and then repeatedly saying "I'm so sorry" for the next week. It just doesn't work that way. You must first acknowledge your fault and then show your partner remorse by correcting the mistake.

Know your reason for doing cardio, and do it for the right reasons. You certainly burn calories but remember that you also burn calories just from sleeping. It's definitely a strategy, but it's not a winning strategy. If you can fully understand this concept, your new outlook on cardio training creates for a more rewarding and enjoyable experience! If you enjoy going on a five mile run because it relieves stress, and you know that you simultaneously build your heart and endurance, then that's amazing! The same goes for going on a hike, swimming, or whatever! Keep doing it. Just don't do it because you feel like you have to burn off that fried chicken and fries you ate for lunch. So again, keep cardiovascular training for heart-related fitness. Control your weight through proper nutrition and your new, healthy lifestyle.

3ʳᵈ Component: Increase Flexibility and ROM (Range of Motion)

To be honest, I never took stretching seriously until I started training in Jiu-Jitsu. I always thought of stretching and flexibility as drudgery and a waste of time. Boy was I wrong. Some say that your flexibility parallels physical wellness. That may not be entirely accurate, but flexibility may be the single most important, yet misunderstood, component of fitness. People with flexibility issues will often experience problems completing any exercise routine.

A lack of flexibility in any muscle can create imbalances throughout your joints (where two bones come together) and eventually throughout the entire body. All of this can lead to dysfunctional movement patterns that eventually cause severe injury. Let's mitigate those chances. Flexibility and your ROM (range of motion) go hand in hand. When people refer to your flexibility, they refer to the ROM surrounding a joint. General guidelines say that muscles account for only 40 percent of joint flexibility. Bones, ligaments, and tendons affect ROM; however, they do not possess characteristics of becoming more flexible.

Make increasing your flexibility and ROM a priority for the remainder of your life. Proper stretching will improve your overall quality of life. Stretching reduces stress, assists in breathing patterns, improves your posture and balance, decreases your chances of injury, and allows for efficient body movements and mechanics.

The following steps should be considered when incorporating flexibility into your new lifestyle:

- Stretch everyday if possible. Utilize every part of the body!
- Drink plenty of water. Keep the body hydrated, as it will make a huge difference.
- Proper Nutrition: The key component to everything! This has a daily cumulative effect.
- Muscles and tendons stretch better when warmed up. Stretch 5-10 minutes after a light aerobic warmup and/or at the end of the training session.
- When stretching, stretch to the point of feeling tension in the muscle—not pain.
- Try to do active stretches (controlled back and forth motion) before your workout and save the static stretches (long hold) for the end of the workout.
- Incorporate Yoga into your routine.
- Buy a foam roller and start foam rolling. This helps loosen up the knots in your body, increases blood flow to your muscles, relieves muscle tension, and helps in increasing your range of motion.

4th Component: Incorporate Martial Arts / Gracie Jiu-Jitsu Into Your Lifestyle

In 2012, I signed up for my first martial arts class. By this time, a lingering knee injury sidelined me from all sports, so I wanted to partake in a physical activity other than weightlifting. I felt nervous because I had never taken up any type of martial art before. Growing up, guys like Bruce Lee and Jean-Claude Van Damme fascinated me with their eye-catching martial arts movies. Today, Mixed Martial Arts or MMA, is one of the fastest growing sports in America. The marketability of the sport continually expands due to the popularity of the Ultimate Fighting Championship (mainly known as the UFC). Due to its utilization in the UFC, I felt excited to deepen my newfound curiosity in Brazilian Jiu-Jitsu. After all, Brazilian Jiu-Jitsu (also known as BJJ) put MMA on the map. I was fired up.

I always knew that the legendary Gracie family brought Brazilian Jiu-Jitsu to the United States; however, I did not know that they interchangeably called it Gracie Jiu-Jitsu. I knew that Royce Gracie popularized this art form back in the 90's when UFC 1 (it is currently UFC 196 as of this book) first aired to the world. As a relatively diminutive and harmless looking fighter, Royce easily destroyed some of the toughest, meanest, and most gargantuan fighters from all over the world. I also knew that the original Gracie Academy opened only two streetlights away from my house in Torrance, CA.

I drove past the Academy daily, as it only took 3-5 minutes from my house! I felt reluctant to go to check it out because I assumed that throughout the years, the academy became too popular and commercialized for my taste. I wanted to do my research so that I could find a lesser known, yet wonderful school with world-class instructors. I must've investigated at least ten different Brazilian Jiu-Jitsu schools until I finally found my school. Four classes later, I was already done! My Brazilian Jiu-Jitsu journey ended. I vividly remember my last day. Just like my first three classes, the first thirty minutes of training involved some sort of calisthenics followed by drilling some moves or movements over and over.

I had no idea what I was doing or why I was even making these moves. Keep in mind that I practiced most of these steps either alone or on a dummy! Then, I would partner up with somebody and again, work on these new moves over and over for another thirty minutes. I dreaded the last thirty minutes. I would spar or fight several students one by one for five minutes each; that's six, competitive rounds of aimless wrestling and grappling for somebody who knew nothing about it!

On my fourth day, I felt completely exhausted and energy depleted after sparring for a few rounds. I wanted to show the upper belts—and the instructors—that I was tough and strong; that though they have better technique, I would give them hell trying to beat me. I wanted to become everybody's nightmare and earn some respect as a new white belt. I hoped to impress everybody with my sheer strength and ability to fight back.

In my last sparring round, I grappled against another guy who signed up recently as well. This guy was much older, out of shape, and about 70 pounds heavier than me. Wonder what old, fat guys do when they roll—especially when they have no skills or technique? They flatten you out and just lay there like a fat pancake and that's exactly what this guy did. I assume he ran out of energy and took advantage of my size so that he can rest. Weighing a little less than 150 pounds, I laid completely lifeless as he plowed on top of me like a heavy wet blanket. I felt so fatigued that my body went limp and I struggled to breathe. He then got up to give me some room and then yelled right in my ear canal, "Come on man! Do something!" For the next few seconds, I tried to fight him off me to no avail.

He broke my spirit and made me feel downright defeated. Then the timer went off. I forced myself up, shook everyone's hands, and walked towards the wall to lie down. I felt nauseous and dizzy, so a kind man sitting next to me offered to share his coconut water. Ten minutes passed and the dojo emptied out when suddenly, my body went into a violent convulsion. My entire body, back, neck, chest, abs, quads, calves and limbs began cramping simultaneously. I looked and felt like Emily Rose. Until this day, I remember it as the most physically painful experience of my life. I nearly called 911 but chose not to because I didn't have insurance.

My body constantly convulsed for the next forty-five minutes. It was horrible. My eyes teared from the pain.

Long story short, I called my sister-in-law to get me from the training facility because I had to make sure that I got home safely—considering my thirty-five mile commute home. Once I got home, the cramping and convulsions flared up again and lasted over an hour! It took my body two full days to recover from that incident. My body could not anticipate the week long beating it took from everybody. I canceled my membership shortly after and decided not to go back. I told the front desk (out of courtesy) that I couldn't commute this far. The saddest part about quitting Brazilian Jiu-Jitsu was that I quit thinking I don't have what it takes to be a martial artist.

Two years later, in mid-2014, Aileen and I went to pick up some groceries from the store. Traffic backed up the street and coincidentally stopped us right next to the entrance of the Gracie Academy. All of a sudden, I turned to Aileen and said, "Hey babe, would you mind if we check out Gracie Academy for a few minutes?" Before she could even answer, I pulled into the parking lot. I drove by this place daily, and since towering bamboo trees surrounded the building, the place looked subtle and quaint. Contrary to my belief, the facility boasted a massive and beautiful space. I mean, what Brazilian Jiu-Jitsu Academy showcases its own dedicated museum? Once we stepped onto the mat area, it felt as if we entered Jiu-Jitsu heaven. As we sat down to observe a class, a man in a gi (kimono) walked over from the other side of the mat to warmly introduce himself. He introduced himself as Danny, and since he wore a multi-striped brown belt, I assumed that he was an instructor welcoming two visitors to the academy. We ended up chit-chatting for about ten minutes and Danny convinced both Aileen and me to take a 10-day free trial.

So why do I explain all of this, and why does the story drag on? Well, first and foremost, I want to be clear that the Gracie Academy or any of their affiliates do not sponsor nor endorse me in any way. They do not in any way or capacity pay me to share this information with you. I'm just another ordinary student who pays tuition just like everybody else. This sport isn't cheap either; however, I know that Gracie Jiu-Jitsu deeply impacted me on a transformational level.

As with every holistic approach I share and everything I stand for in life, I view Gracie Jiu-Jitsu as a personal transformation. It develops character and promotes respect, discipline, and empowerment. From baseball and basketball to tennis and volleyball, I played competitive sports my entire life. I competed in recreational leagues or for club teams all the way up until my 30's—when a torn ACL and meniscus sidelined me from competition. Even though my injury cut my competitive career short, I will always carry the drive and values of a competitor every day. I don't think the hunger to win and compete ever leaves you.

Today, I could never imagine that Gracie Jiu-Jitsu would become a lifestyle for both Aileen and I; that this art form (I don't want to call it a sport) would superlatively impact my life more than all those years of playing sports combined. I now consider The Gracie Academy my second home. My head instructors, Ryron and Rener Gracie, both founded the Gracie University. They are the grandsons of Helio Gracie, the creator of Gracie Jiu-Jitsu, and the sons of Rorion Gracie, the person responsible for bringing Gracie Jiu-Jitsu to the United States.

While Helio and Rorion Gracie introduced Gracie Jiu-Jitsu to the world by co-founding and creating the Ultimate Fighting Championship (yes, UFC), Ryron and Rener spread the gospel by establishing Gracie Certified Training Centers around the world. In addition, their instructional DVD's and internet content make the art form more accessible to people worldwide. The brothers also created Gracie University: the first interactive, online martial arts learning center. With more than 125,000 active online students spanning across 196 different countries, the program offers custom-tailored self-defense programs for men, women, and children. It is legit! I enjoy seeing some of the best UFC fighters on the planet like Ronda Rousey and Lyoto Machida come through and train at the academy on a regular basis. I am even more fired up witnessing my own instructor, Brian T-City Ortega, climb up UFC's featherweight division where I believe he will be a champion one day. I see NFL stars, famous actors, and musicians call the Gracie Academy home as well. It's an incredible community and a life-learning platform for everyone.

I talk about Gracie Jiu-Jitsu so much because they create accessible online programs for anybody. Also, Gracie Certified Training Centers—all across the world and the United States—share the same Gracie curriculum. Even if you do not live anywhere near these certified training centers or feel that the online information or DVD's do not suffice, by all means, please find the nearest Jiu-Jitsu school near you.

My point is, have you found your Gracie Jiu-Jitsu? By this, I mean that this journey can come in the form of another martial arts establishment such as Krav Maga, Muay Thai, Tae Kwon Do, or even Yoga. Just find a place that focuses on developing your transformational growth. Be mindful of establishments that place an emphasis on building the next champion cage fighter. Many of these institutions serve as a breeding ground for medals and trophies; these schools focus more on creating and marketing their reputation. If you want to become the next UFC champion, then by all means pick a school that brings up the best fighters. Just like bodybuilders and fitness enthusiasts, the best martial arts practitioners sync with their art physically, mentally, and spiritually. Take your martial arts training and be a life practitioner. Learning techniques in self-defense enhances your transformational journey.

5TH COMPONENT: ATTITUDE OF GRATITUDE

When you master the first four elements of this step, what do you get? Tremendous results. Gratitude accompanies excellent results. Charles Schwab said, "The way to develop the best that is in a person is by appreciation and encouragement." When I first started Jiu-Jitsu training, my friend, Clifton, who trained for many years told me to look at my goal through *the 1 percent rule*. He explained that each day, I should try to improve my technique and knowledge by 1 percent. That's not asking too much, but if you can do that, then after one month of training, you will have improved by 10%. Thank you Clifton ☺

When you train right, eat right, and encourage others in the process, you will reach your goals the right way: by improving at least 1% each day. You learn to appreciate the entire process: eating foods based on how they impact your body, being grateful for your exercise equipment and training facilities, and inspiring others with your sense of leadership. Your attitude of gratitude becomes the permanent bridge to growth and transformation.

Fitness and Martial Arts is a privilege and a gift. Your mind possesses the most power and your body forges into the world's greatest weapon. When you use your body correctly, it becomes unstoppable. Be grateful for your body, for this type of gratitude empowers you and takes you to the next level. When gratitude leads the way, it opens up the door for more gratifying activities.

Chapter 4
Step 4: Master Your Wealth & Success

"Wealth is the ability to fully experience life."
—**Henry David Thoreau**

1st Component: Belief & Mindset

The amount of money you currently make reflects your monetary beliefs. Jack Ma, the founder of Alibaba (the world's biggest online e-commerce company), possess a net worth of $26 billion. He said that if you're still poor at 35, you deserve it. This quote stung me a bit because I remember being 35 and feeling as though I trailed in wealth and success. I'm not sure if *deserve* best describes my feelings; however, I realized that my beliefs towards money situated me in my current position. Les Brown said, "The easiest thing I've ever done was to earn a million dollars. The most difficult thing I've ever done was to believe it could happen to me. That was the most difficult part – TO BELIEVE."

I had to redefine my relationship with money because I grew up in an environment where money, or lack of, broke up my family. For the longest time, I struggled with money. Growing up with a poor mindset put me face to face with many negative voices. As I look back, my grandparents passed this poor mentality down to my parents, who in turn, passed it down to me. So what did I do? I stopped caring about money and decided not to care about being rich or poor. I soon realized that this philosophy didn't work either. Today, I understand that money gives me more opportunities to give back. Money is a vehicle for the right kind of empowerment.

Here's my main point: It makes better sense to disconnect money from wealth. Wealth allows you to fully experience life! Wealth does not equal money. Wealth is a mindset. Poverty is also a mindset. Differentiate *wealth* from being *financially free* and *poor* from being *broke*. *Wealth* and *poverty* contribute to two different states of mind, but being *financially free* and *being broke* represents physical circumstances. Being financially free means that you no longer have to work or trade time for money. Being broke, well, I'm sure I don't need to explain that.

Now that I've made those distinctions, let me ask you: do you financially work out? Are you financially fit? Just like all of our previous steps, the same principles apply to building wealth: it begins and ends in the mind. Here's a kicker—when it comes to wealth, stop trying so hard. Make it your priority to master your money; don't let your money master you. A lot of people attain financial freedom, but by that time, they lose their health, relationships, and their identity.

Throughout my life, I experienced both poverty and financial benediction. I prefer the latter! I'm able to go on nice vacations with Aileen, host a lot of barbecues at our house, and share my blessings with others. More importantly, I enjoy the fruits of my labor, and I no longer feel guilty about working hard and making good money. The more I make, the more I contribute and make a difference. No matter what, I will always choose to live a great life. Choose happiness first because if you live an excellent life, you cannot fear a regretful death. A life well spent is more meaningful than a life full of money. With money, you must obtain a proper vision, establish the proper mindset, and then commit to achieving your daily financial goals. I understand that any day, I can lose all my money and go broke; however, I will never be poor because *poor* refers to a state of mind.

2ND COMPONENT: PASSION & PURPOSE

My existence requires me to build the kings and queens of the next generation. To me, happiness and living out my passion—while staying true to myself—creates the highest platform of success. Nobody can take that away from me, and nobody can place a price on that. Even with all that I do, I live the happiest life; however, it wasn't always this way. Money and fame wrapped me up for a few years, and I chased it hard. In 2009, a couple of buddies and I lost a little over $100K investing into my former band manager's clothing line. I vowed not to chase money after that.

Today, making money no longer consumes me. Instead, I obsess over learning something new every day. I concentrate on creating freedom for my family and creating opportunities for others, and guess what? I make more money than I have ever earned before. My friends acknowledge Aileen and me as the couple who travel all the time. People always ask me why do I wake up so early and do what I repeatedly do? I respond by telling them that I know my life's passion and purpose and that I wish to die a meaningful death—knowing that my work here is done.

You must love what you do. I believe a life of progress consists of living out your dreams and being happy. Furthermore, you cannot find a way toward passion; it must be the way. You also cannot find a way to happiness as happiness itself is the way. Let your passion rule, and watch as the rest follows in accord. When you do what you love most, the money ultimately follows. So, what are you most passionate about? What would you do on your day off? The answer to that should be your life's work.

In 2011, Aileen and I decided to dedicate our lives to serving and helping others. Many moons ago, my grandfather founded a non-profit organization called the

"Better Living Center" near Downtown Los Angeles. For the past 40+ years, this 50-unit boarding house assisted less fortunate individuals in starting a new life. This center housed them, fed them, and developed their skills and mindsets. Recently, my grandfather broke into his late 80's. He lacked the energy and resources needed to run his non-profit, so he asked me to take over. Aileen and I jubilantly accepted the opportunity to fulfill our passion. We developed a plan and set monstrous goals.

Since the 50-unit property spanned across an entire block, we possessed enough land to build a fitness center, a small theater (for speaking events and programs), and an aquaponics system (for growing a self-sustaining tilapia farm and vegetable garden). After Aileen and I had married, we both quit our jobs and went on a two-month trip to Asia. It was our way of getting out with the old and in with the new. When we came back, we teamed up with another group so that we can co-brand our new non-profit organization. Three months into our planning, both sides could not come to an agreement as too many formidable obstacles arose that abruptly aborted our mission. The other group parted ways and the Board of Directors for my grandfather's non-profit organization decided to sell the property.

Aileen and I felt devastated. We were unemployed newlyweds who exhausted all of our savings traveling across Asia. We inched down to our last few dollars and our situation forced us to move back in with my mother. We started back at ground zero and let me tell you that was a tough pill to swallow. Luckily, Aileen found a position as an assistant, and this $17 per hour wage supported the both of us through the following year. Can you imagine how I felt as a man, and as a new husband? Despite the excruciating pain, we always found a way toward our passion and purpose. Aileen supported me even as I refused to get an ordinary job. Within 18 months, I became certified as a Personal Trainer, Nutritionist, and Life Coach. After earning my real estate license, the arduous journey of building my business began. Every day, I felt like the biggest loser on the planet. My wife supported me on a $17/hr salary while we lived at my mom's house.

I felt so bad for putting Aileen in this position. On our nationally televised wedding, I promised her parents that I would take care of her; now that overwhelming guilt killed me, and I felt like the biggest liar. I distinctly remember waking up next to Aileen: my alarm would ring at 4 A.M., and I would cuddle her for a bit before heading out. I hated myself for not being able to support her. You couldn't even imagine my forty-minute commute to the gym. I would wear my sunglasses so nobody can see me cry. Once I got to the gym's parking lot, I would wipe off all my tears, say a quick prayer, and head off to train my clients.

I continued grinding for two years until I finally started making a profit. My real estate career flourished alongside my fitness business. Today, I think back to the days when I cried myself to work; I tear up just thinking about it. I pride myself on persevering through those tough moments. I read this just yesterday that, "...Perseverance is more than endurance. It is endurance combined with absolute assurance and certainty that what we are looking for is going to happen." I persevered because I knew my passion and my purpose.

3rd Component: Have Great Mentors and Be a Great Mentor

One of my favorite books is *The Book of Five Rings*. This story follows the journey of Musashi Miyamoto, one of the greatest and most noble Samurai warriors to ever walk the Earth. Miyamoto inculcated the belief that, "just as one man can defeat ten, so a hundred men can defeat a thousand, and a thousand can defeat ten thousand." I interpret Miyamoto's quote as, "just as one can help ten, so a hundred can help a thousand, and a thousand can help ten thousand."

I consult different mentors for each area of my life. These instructors hold me accountable for my personal growth and guide me through the journey toward overall wellness. When people think of mentors, they imagine a successful guru who carves out similar paths for their apprentices. I believe that mentors act as servant leaders: someone who shares power, prioritizes others, and assists people in reaching their highest potential. Mentoring actively partners you with an expert who guides your deliberate, personal transformation. Be specific about who you want mentoring you because mentoring does not solely translate into teaching and transferring skills; it establishes a relationship that builds and develops reciprocally.

A mentor uses their leadership skills to provide empowering insight. They should understand and share your visions and dreams. They should not only motivate and inspire, but also help direct people toward their unique greatness. They provide you with tools and tasks that build upon your potential. A real mentor is honest and truthful.

Be a Mentor

Transformation transpires through a process of owning personal responsibility. In the US, the average CEO's tenure lasts about 14 months; they are public enemy number 2. Do you know who tops the list? Elected politicians. We live in a world where people distrust their leaders. If you become a leader, you automatically alienate people, and that's why mentors must master the art of relations.

As a life coach and mentor, I develop the framework for my client's life. I wish that my mentees become more successful than me because breeding success exemplifies the greatest joy of my work. My style or personality may not cater to everyone, and that's okay. My job revolves around showing you your life. I want you to work towards a commitment as you simultaneously discover your voice.

4th Component: Take Appropriate Risk, Fail Fast, and Maximize Opportunity Today!

Let's be honest with ourselves. You don't get out of life alive; you die sooner than you think. For that reason alone, you must take appropriate risks that maximize your opportunities. My mentor, Hendre, always says, "Take risks and fail fast." He taught me that life bestows the greatest gifts to those who take chances. Keep in mind though, that taking risks doesn't equate to jeopardizing money or endangering business opportunities.

Have you attended a party and never talked to anyone? You probably left that event early, right? Now think about a time when you went to a party and met new people; it was fun, exciting, and scary all at the same time, right? Research indicates that the brain handles risk better than ambiguity. This disparity occurs because people get tripped up by analysis paralysis. Free yourself from the apathy and start taking some chances. This philosophy may not change your life; however, it may build your momentum going forward. In regards to improving your current situation, who can you reach out to and ask for help? Who can provide guidance toward a better path? What's preventing you from opening more opportunities? When we procrastinate, we kill our plans. Listen, I'm not here to provoke guilt; I'm here to get you moving!

The best mentors and influencers steered into my life when I began to take risks. I did not know these people during my rock star days, nor did I associate with them throughout college. Taking risks and failing forward opened up endless opportunities. If we fail to take risks, we fail to truly live.

The seven strong factors below identify whether or not you take appropriate risks.

1. Passion (pain of sacrifice)
2. Experiencing failures /resistance from others / when people tell you it's "risky"
3. Innovation / Collaboration
4. Being out of your comfort zone
5. Having a clear vision
6. Agility /Adaptability
7. Fun / Excitement

I loved reading John Maxwell's book, *Failing Forward*. It will go down as one of my favorite books, and I revisit it often. Whenever I experience a setback or failure, reading a few pages helps me recalibrate my mental toughness. The book redefines the world *fail*. Today, failing at something means that I progress toward a breakthrough and that I inch one step closer to my goals. I actually get excited when things do not work out the way I planned. Taken directly out of his book, Maxwell emphasizes these fifteen points.

1. Realize there is one major difference between average people and achieving people.
2. Learn a new definition of failure.
3. Remove the 'you' from failure.
4. Take action and reduce your fear.
5. Change your response to failure by accepting responsibility.
6. Don't let the failure from outside get inside you.
7. Say good-bye to yesterday.
8. Change yourself, and your world changes.
9. Get over yourself and start giving yourself.
10. Find the benefit in every bad experience.
11. If at first you do succeed, try something harder.
12. Learn from a bad experience and make it a good experience.
13. Work on the weakness that weakens you.
14. Understand there's not much difference between success and failure.
15. Get up, get going, and get over it.

Regarding personal finances, my friend, Attorney Mark Smith, outlined an effective strategy for taking appropriate risks and maximizing profits.

Everything you need to know about financial planning (From Dilbert and the Way of the Weasel, 2002.)

1. Make a will.
2. Pay off your credit cards.

3. Get term life insurance if you have a family to support.
4. Fund your 401k to the maximum.
5. Fund your IRA to the maximum.
6. Buy a house if you want to live in a house and you can afford it.
7. Put six months' expenses in a money market fund.
8. Take whatever money is left over and invest 70% in a stock index fund and 30% in a bond fund through any discount broker and never touch it until retirement.
9. If any of this confuses you, or have something special going on (retirement, college planning, tax issues), hire a fee-based financial planner, not one who charges a percentage of your portfolio.

As I've mentioned earlier in this book, I love "The Book of Five Rings" by Musashi Miyamoto. In his book, Miyamoto analyzes personal struggle and self-mastery from a multitude of angles. He explains *the way* and shares applicable tools for undergoing a transformational process. Here they are:

1. Do not be dishonest.
2. Training reveals the way (life of progress).
3. Familiarize yourself with all the arts .
4. Familiarize yourself with all the skills.

5. Distinguish between gain and loss in worldly matters.
6. Hone your instincts.
7. Sense what you cannot see.
8. Notice even the obscure.
9. Do not waste time and do nothing that is of no use.

5th Component: Gratitude and Integrity

Build your wealth honestly and with integrity. Do not be envious of other people's success and do not hate on your friends who make more money than you. Celebrate the success of your competitors because it'll free you. If you hate on successful people, you will fail to become successful. Today's gratitude buys you tomorrow's happiness, so express your gratitude for success and praise successful people. Your time will come, believe me. You will succeed. Having integrity in your life's work allows you to develop your true character throughout the process of transformation. Presenting your true self allows you to undergo a real transformation.

Social media makes it easy to lose sight of your own progress. We become entangled in other people's lives, as we sit back and passively observe society through Facebook, Instagram, or YouTube. We develop such a deep interest in other people's lives that we forget about our own personal progression! I believe that people use social media to express their true selves. Social media platforms actualize people's inner conversations and for some, this form of expression can work against them. When companies consider hiring a future employee, do you think that they check the candidate's social media? Absolutely!

People (mainly your friends) who consistently post content on social media typically exude the complete opposite characteristics in their personal lives. You know what I'm talking about. Listen, social media does not translate into true reality. People's reality, especially through social media, does not parallel your reality. At the end of the day, social media acts as a connecting platform. What you do solitarily and what you do offline determines your level of success, so do the work and do it well. You will not get results by dodging hard work. Stay true to your core.

Remember, how you do anything defines how you do everything. Having integrity and gratitude means living life to your full potential. That's integrity; that defines success and happiness. No amount of money will ever surpass that feeling. Don't worry about branding yourself to the world. You build your brand upon your results and your efforts. When you succeed with integrity and gratitude, you find your real voice and no longer feel the need to speak up or show off. You no longer yearn to post misleading pictures that symbolize your success and happiness because you free yourself from that. As you exercise your gratitude and develop your 10-10-10's, you begin to fall in love with life.

You will even grow to appreciate death because mortality enhances integrity and honesty. When we die, we wish to be remembered as someone who did things right; someone who treated people with integrity. Integrity is what you do when nobody is watching. Jim Rohn said it best, "True inspiration should never be conscious of itself." This humbling quote blows me away. I hope you utilize this state of mind as you progress forward.

Chapter 5
Step 5: Master of Giving

> *"No-one has become poor by giving."*
> **—Anne Frank**

1st Component: Give = Forgive

What does it mean to forgive? When you forgive, you allow yourself to commit again. Over time, you become what you are unwilling to forgive. Right now, think of all the things that make you reluctant to forgive. Is your unwillingness to forgive evident in your behaviors?

For the longest time, I did not forgive my father. Growing up, I viewed my dad as my hero; I always aimed to make him proud. We formed a very special bond by playing sports together. Even after coming home from work, he would find time to play catch with me, throw the football around, or shoot some hoops together in the back yard. He was awesome.

When I was 10 years old, he shattered my world. My father told my family that he planned on moving to Japan—leaving me, my mom, and my sister behind. My parents clearly did not get along as financial difficulties exploded many of our domestic issues. At times, it got so ugly that I remember seeing objects fly across the living room; one time my dad even flipped the living room piano onto the floor. Every day my parents' irreconcilable differences grew more evident. Rather than filing for a divorce, my father took a teaching job overseas. This new position offered a much higher pay and he hoped that this split would diffuse some tension between him and my mom.

I remember my dad promised me that since his teaching contract lasted only a year, he would return in no time. I still remember watching him disappear into the airport's terminal; a piece of me died that day. I never felt the same after that. As a ten-year old child, I felt that my dad abandoned me. I assumed he didn't love me enough to want to stay. This void consumed me all throughout my childhood.

As the one-year mark approached, I couldn't wait for his return. I felt stoked to have my dad back! Within a few days of his expected arrival, my father told us that the school extended his contract for another year, and once again, my world crumbled. For the past year, I crossed off each calendar day as I anxiously waited for his arrival. After two years he told us that the company, again, extended his contract. This process repeated itself as two years became three, and three became four.

Twenty-seven years have passed since my dad left for Japan. Ironically, just a few days ago, he sent me an email letting me know that his school finally decided not to renew his contract due to his age. The school does not employ anyone over the age of 65. As I reflect, I can't believe that I am 37 years old— the same age as my father when he left. I feel my emotions roar as I write this. Twenty-seven years passed in a blink of an eye.

To this day, I deeply regret telling my dad that I didn't give a crap whether he attended my wedding or not. He missed out on all the important events throughout my life, so why was this any different? I told him that his absence taught me how to be a man, and I also blamed him for all of my anger and my zealous temper tantrums. I indicted him for that insecure chip on my shoulder. I exuded bitterness everywhere. CS Lewis said, "Bitterness is drinking poison, expecting somebody else to die." Part of my personal transformation involved learning how to forgive.

Forgiveness does not include justifying other people's behavior. It doesn't mean, "it's okay that my father abandoned me because his father abandoned him." You cannot use forgiveness to excuse somebody's behaviors. You cannot rape or abuse people just because it happened to you. Forgiveness does not condone injustice.

My mentor, Hendre, played a pivotal role in helping me forgive my dad. We tend to think of forgiveness as an act instead of an attitude; yet, who suffers when you live life unforgivably? Your wife, your husband, your partner, your siblings, friends, and business partners. It's not fair to them. Forgiveness does not require reconciliation. Exonerating someone does not set them free; instead, it sets you free. Release yourself from that burden and start giving once again.

Remember, you become what you are unwilling to forgive. Hendre slammed me with the question, "Cary, when are you going to stop being the boy whose father never came back?" You see, I can't take responsibility for my dad's actions, but I certainly can accept responsibility for my feelings and my reactions. When I adopted this point of view, my father's abandonment no longer owned me. I acknowledge my painful past; however, I freed myself from those restraints so that I can form a new relationship with my dad. In a few months, he'll be back for good. He may arrive by the time you guys read this book. It's scary, but I'm excited, and I'm ready. I thank God that nothing tragic took place during my time of bitterness. Sometimes, you must take care of yourself before you can start giving. I love my father wholeheartedly because I no longer hold him to the standard of the ideal dad. Forgiveness equals freedom. Forgive = For / GIVE. Forgiving is for giving again. That's deep. ☺

2ND COMPONENT: GIVE YOUR MONEY

Money can grab you whether you have it or not. If you feel that money commands you—start giving. As Luke 6:38 says, "Give, and it shall be given to you." There's a difference between handing everything away and acting as a good steward of your blessing. The Bible tells us to give. How much? 10%. Does God need 10% of your money? No. Do you think God says, "Hey Cary, it's been a pretty difficult month for me, can you spare me 10% of your earnings this time?"

Contributing this 10% sets you free. The act of giving symbolizes the beginning of your freedom. In "The Game of Life and How to Play it," Florence S. Shinn says, "Giving opens the way of receiving. In order to create activity in finances, one should give. Tithing or giving one-tenth of one's income, is an old Jewish custom, and is sure to bring an increase. Many of the richest men in this country have been tithers, and I have never known it to fail as an investment…Bills should be paid cheerfully; all money should be sent forth fearlessly and with a blessing. This attitude of mind makes man master of money. It is his to obey, and his spoken word then opens a vast reservoir of wealth." Give your money to somebody who can do something with it. Giving to the poor and the needy is okay, but should you also give money to someone who is wealthy? Or, how about a well-established organization? Of course, you can because giving shows that you believe in their cause. Free yourself from a poor mindset and give 10%.

3RD COMPONENT: GIVE YOUR TIME

Time is life's most valuable possession. No matter how hard we try, we cannot escape death. With every clock strike forward, we lose time to our mortality. Despite this impermanent feeling, people *spend* their time doing things, as if it's expendable. Let us change the phrase *spending time* to *get to give our time*. You see, people realize whether you *spend* time with them, or *give* them time. You change your relationship with time when you look at it through another perspective.

When I train Jiu-Jitsu, I give my time to the Gracie Academy. I also *give* my time by assisting two beginner's Jiu-Jitsu classes per week. I look forward to this and absolutely love it! Due to my dreadful experience as a white belt, I prioritize the students' enjoyment as a new practitioner. I don't want them to feel threatened, out of place, weak, or defeated because those feelings once forced me to abandon Jiu-Jitsu. Giving my time at the dojo corresponds to my life's purpose—to build the kings and queens of our next generation. I feel extremely passionate about *giving* my time rather than *spending* it.

Time entraps people more than money does. "I would like to go there but I don't have time. I'd like to be in a relationship but I don't have time." Liar! You suffer from fear. For the faith-based people, how much time should you dedicate to God? One day out of seven. They call this day the Sabbath. God requests that people rest from sunset to sunset, so that they can spend the next 24 hours with family and loved ones. When you rest, you develop a different relationship with time. Your relationship to time outweighs your relationship to money. Giving your time to connect with people is hard work!

Try turning yourself off for one day. Can you spend 24 hours with your phone completely off? People have lost the ability to talk to one another, so probably not—right? Due to our newfound dependence on cell phones and social media, we lay defenseless to a socially awkward time period. People share their time together by watching TV. If you disconnect yourself from digital media, you realize how unaccustomed we've become to human interaction. I find it funny when people act surprised over failed relationships.

Giving your time requires work. Fortunately, you can give your time through multiple facets. Give time to your family, charity, church, and loved ones and learn to connect there first. You will find the real meaning of commitment, devotion, and faith. In addition, your conflict resolution skill will develop immensely. For all you lovers out there, you get to give your time making love rather than spending time having sex. In recent years, several of my friends told me that having kids restricts their sex life to one session per month! One friend even mentioned that he's lucky to get it twice a year! This is not acceptable, folks. I believe that sex enables you to create more love, so make love as much as you can!

4TH COMPONENT: GIVE YOUR BETRAYAL

We all experience betrayal at some point in our lives, and dealing with it can crush you. Sometimes we betray others, ourselves, and (if you're a believer) God. What you do with this betrayal and how you recount it, will determine how far you can advance your potential.

This betrayal can strangle you. To be free from money you must give money. To be free from time, you must give time. Guess what you do with betrayal? Yep, you get to give it. We use betrayal as a way to justify our behaviors; however, we will now use betrayal as a way to serve others. For example, people empower themselves by sharing their darkest secrets—using it as a tool to transform.

I personally like to forget betrayals. Would you like to forget the things someone did to you or the things you did to someone else? I for sure know I do. Why do we want to forget these acts of betrayal? I want to forget because I want my life back! I yearn for the comfort of a settled mind. When you betray someone or when someone betrays you, that memory serves as a point of reference. You start to look at everything through a fearful perspective. You see your potential, but then the memory of betrayal interferes with your point of view. You want to move toward your capabilities; however, as you inch closer, your betrayal shouts louder and immobilizes your progress.

From now on, own your betrayal and don't identify yourself through that odious act. Ditch the casualties and declare a new identity. I remember betraying people and people betraying me, but instead of burying these guilts, I exposed them to the light and declared my new reality. From now on, I want you to choose a life of freedom. I will be a husband, I will be a son, a brother, and a friend, and I will be faithful, devoted, and committed. Usher away your betrayals and you will get your life back.

5TH COMPONENT: LEAD & SERVE UNCONDITIONALLY.

By the time you complete this book, you will realize that the world does not center upon you. You learn to value your life based on how you impact the world. Find your life's work and directly or indirectly touch the lives of others. Your vision and purpose supersede you because this forms your legacy.

It's been said that everything rises and falls on leadership, and the best type of leader, is a servant leader. For me, my life as a kingmaker includes serving my family, my loved ones, my clients, and everyone and anyone unconditionally.

When the grim reaper knocks on my door, I find comfort in knowing that my work here is finished. It all comes around full circle. Again, I'll ask you, what would you want written on your gravestone?

You don't have to answer *yes* to everything while serving unconditionally because that just makes you a pushover. A servant leader empowers others to do the unthinkable. Encourage others toward an extraordinary life filled with inspired action. Unconditional servitude requires inspiration, and true inspiration lacks consciousness. A servant leader focuses on the greater good of the group and the community. Let's be clear about this though. You can act as a leader, yet fail to effectively lead. Hitler was a powerful leader, but unfortunately his leadership opposed the kind the world wanted or needed. It's the amalgamation of these two transcending qualities that produce the essence of transformation.

Stanford University offered my Jiu-Jitsu instructor and mentor, Rener Gracie, a full scholarship in wrestling and academics. When you meet him, you cannot deny his intellect, enormous personality, and passion to teach. He possesses the characteristics of a Fortune 500 CEO. He passed on his Stanford scholarship so that he could take Gracie Jiu-Jitsu to the next level. He explained in one interview, "The Gracie plan will not be accomplished in one lifetime." Martial artists now practice Gracie Jiu-Jitsu in over 195 countries and Rener's role as a servant leader contributed to that.

Don't be conscious of it; people can immediately sense your intentions. Jim Rohn once told his audience, "be so busy recognizing others that you no longer need it for yourself." Your life and growth equip you toward a life of gratitude. If not, the people around you will always provide compliments and feedback. This support system advances you through life.

Be a servant leader for your family, friends, co-workers, business partners, church members, jiu-jitsu community, etc. Your world will change, and more importantly the world around you will change. I can't wait to see your life transform in front of your eyes. People will naturally gravitate towards you, and The Law of Attraction will forcefully exert itself. Everything I've covered in this book will actualize into your life. Brendon Burchard, a leading online motivational speaker and author explains that the three most important questions a person asks themselves when it comes down to life is, "1. Did I live? 2. Did I love? 3. Did I matter?" You will easily answer these three by the time your life's done.

Chapter 6
FINAL WORDS

"It is better to be prepared and not have an opportunity than to have an opportunity and not be prepared."
— **Les Brown**

This past weekend, the world witnessed one of the most anticipated fights in UFC history (UFC 196). Conor McGregor, the current Featherweight Champion (as of this writing this book), jumped up two weight classes (from 145lbs to 170) to fight Nate Diaz, a UFC journeyman, and veteran fighter. The lines heavily favored McGregor as he took this opportunity to become the only UFC fighter in history to concurrently hold two championship belts in two different weight classes. McGregor is the face of the UFC and fans often mention him among the greatest mixed martial artists of our day. Diaz, on the other hand, accepted the fight with a brief 11-day notice, so nobody thought that Diaz could win. Experts from all around explained that

Diaz's lack of preparation versus a champion fighter would only expedite his defeat.

Though Diaz took an early beating, he managed to take the brash, trash-talking McGregor into the 2nd round. Just when it looked like Dana White would once again raise McGregor's arm, the gritty Diaz began to turn the tides in his favor. Shockingly, he out struck McGregor and forced him to the ground where he used his polished Jiu-Jitsu skills to finish him off. Victim to a rear naked choke hold, McGregor lied lifeless in the cage while Diaz jubilantly danced from corner to corner.

The announcer, Joe Rogan, came running toward Diaz for the post fight interview. He commented that Diaz achieved the impossible—that he shocked the world. Diaz won the biggest fight of his career with nearly zero preparation. Rogan then asked Diaz if the outcome surprised him. Diaz grabbed the microphone and then shouted, "I'm not surprised Motherf*****s! I've been fighting in the UFC for over ten years! We all have to be prepared to fight on any given day, and I'll fight anybody, anywhere, and I don't care about any belt." In another post-fight interview, Diaz further explained that on his absolute worst days, he would still train for at least 2 hours a day—preparing himself to fight at any time. Ten years ago, when he entered the UFC, he decided to become a vegan. Diaz wanted to be in the best shape of his life throughout his entire fighting career. For many years, Diaz pursued the mastery of his craft and just eleven days before the biggest

Pay Per View fight in UFC history, the UFC counted on him to rise to the occasion. His shocking upset over Conor McGregor also resulted in the biggest payday of his life—a whopping $620,000!

A time will come when greatness calls upon you, so take that opportunity and display your greatness. I hope to either be there or hear about it when it goes down. Les Brown said, "It is better to be prepared and not have an opportunity than to have an opportunity and not be prepared." Dave Ramsey said, "If you live like no one else, later you can live like no one else." Do the work and be prepared. I believe that one day, the world will recognize me as one of the most respected and influential Transformation Specialists and speakers in the world. My relentless dedication, preparation, and commitment guided me through my arduous journey—landing me where I am today.

As I write these closing remarks, I find it hard to believe that over 30 days ago, I challenged myself into writing my first book. On top of that, I set a goal to get it published in 90 days! I hired a coaching team, wrote out a contract, and posted it on my wall in front of my desk. I also discussed my goal with a handful of trusted friends—just for accountability purposes. I plastered a calendar to my wall and promised to write a minimum of 2-hours every single day for the next 30 days. I don' think I wrote a perfect book, but I still finished it. It's been a tough 30 days, and I've had to make some changes. Typically, I turned off my phone for

12 hours out of the day. I told Aileen that she cannot contact me during certain hours, as I hopped from coffee shop to coffee shop.

I have always dreamed of writing a book, but I thought becoming an author might elude me. Over the years, I shared my aspirations with a few people, mentioning that I would write a book before I die. Despite my desires, I never expected that this day would come. I thought of it as a dream, and I would always hear other people say the same thing, "Yeah, I want to write a book too!" Well, it gives me great joy that I can now call myself an author. I share this book with you so that you know what you can do. I never thought I'd be the one saying this, but whatever you put your mind to, you can accomplish. Your greatness awaits you! I can reassure you that many amazing things wait for you on the other side of your commitment; however, it'll only work if you participate and engage. Own your self, rise to the challenge, and you will find true inner peace. Make sure to live an extraordinary life full of inspired action, regardless of your circumstances. I hope to hear from you soon!

Lightning Source UK Ltd.
Milton Keynes UK
UKHW020214081019
351174UK00003B/63/P